Thirteen Moons More
Andi Webb

PROLOGUE

'How did we come to be?'

"I ignored your aura but it grabbed me by the hand, like the moon pulled the tide, and the tide pulled the sand."

— Talib Kweli

Welcome to my family. I am Andi, I'm gay, and I've been a stay-at-home dad for over five years now. I live with my long-term partner, John, two crazy Dalmatians, and five children under the age of six.

John and I actually met - for one night only - some twenty-five years ago in a very well-known gay bar in West London. Thinking back to those times they seem a world away from where we are today! After meeting again in 1995 we became an item, and three years later we moved into our first home together in Hammersmith. We were both working very hard, having started our two separate businesses, and before we knew it another few years had passed. We began to hanker after the patter of tiny paws, and finally, in 2008, we chose a Dalmatian puppy, a beautiful little boy that we called Remus.

After officially being a couple for thirteen years we had finally become a family!

Despite our good intentions, Remus ultimately managed to gain access to the bed and the bigger he got, the more we were pushed to the sides. Three years later Remus fathered a litter of puppies and we were gifted one of them, a little girl that we called Gracie; we hadn't planned on getting another one, and the very handsome Gracie became part of our slowly expanding family.

There were a few small instances that led to the realisation that we could father our own children. The first one for me was, if Remus could manage it, well, why couldn't we? We're fairly intelligent people and if you plan for something carefully, most things are possible, aren't they? However, the main epiphany was a late-night program on television. Channel-surfing for something to watch, I came across 'Made in India'. It told the story of a heterosexual couple and their journey through IVF, resulting in a third-party surrogate carrying their genetic child to term. The surrogate was well paid, the clinic was well paid, and the result was one happy family! Now, at that time we had all heard of celebrity surrogacies like Elton John and David Furness having a baby. So, I thought, what is so different from John and me using an egg donor (much like sperm donation) and a surrogate to carry the child?

I spent a week researching, checking and rechecking facts, and when I finally, apprehensively, excitedly, broached the subject with John, we realised that we both wanted the same thing: to become fathers.

It took over a year to negotiate the tangle of red tape in India, where we chose to have our first surrogacy; the laws were strict in both India and the UK, and finding a woman who met all the criteria took time. It was John and me who planned the family and to be the sole parents; the egg donor wasn't planning on being a mother to our children and as for the surrogate? She wasn't doing this for us to be nice; we chose Compensated Surrogacy in India (not legal here in the UK) and she was very well paid to carry our twin babies to term. There was no genetic connection. Our children only have two parents and we both happen to be men! So, thirty-five weeks later, in March 2013, we became a family of two dads, two spotty dogs and now, two little baby girls. The family was growing, but the twins were eight months old before we managed to get the necessary paperwork to bring them back to the UK.

We discussed what we would call ourselves, mulled it over, and eventually agreed that John would be Daddy and I would be Dadda. Later he would tell me that he was a little bit jealous, because babies say Dadda long before they say Daddy.

It was some time before fortune blessed us with our next child, baby Thor. In fact, he was conceived on or around the girls first birthday, but they would have to wait another nine months (and some) to receive the gift of a little brother. India was closed to us as an option as the country had changed its laws surrounding surrogacy, so Thor was born in late December 2014 in Thailand - just before Thailand also changed its laws regarding surrogacy! It took another few months to organise the required paperwork and bring the baby home.

During this time the family was split into two and I missed John and the girls more than I can say. John coped with them both with the help of his sister, Sara, and a live-in au pair. During this time John had enrolled the twins in a preschool in the mornings. When I came home with Thor, we decided to surprise the girls; I strapped Thor to my chest in the baby sling and went to pick them up. When they skipped out and saw me and baby Thor, they both screamed, 'Dadda, Dadda,' and hurled themselves at me, throwing their arms around my legs. I was so happy to see them, both taller and so much more grown-up than when I had gone away. We were now a family of two dads, two spotty dogs, two girls and a little bolt of thunder named Thor. Well, three children down and just the final two to go.

I didn't mention earlier that we had had a few failures when it came to getting pregnant; three no-starter pregnancies and two miscarriages. We expected our next attempt at pregnancy would probably be unsuccessful, so even before Thor was born, we made another attempt and assumed we would have to try again six months down the line.

You can imagine our surprise when we learned that our first attempt had been successful, and then our absolute shock when, soon afterwards, we discovered that we were to have another set of twins! On this occasion our children would be born at the top of the world, under the shadow of Mount Everest. We would very soon become a family of two dads, two spotty dogs, two sets of beautiful twins and a little bolt of thunder who went by the name of Thor.

Aaliyah and Caleb were born in Nepal, in July 2015, just after the devastating earthquake of April 2015 in which nearly 9000 people lost their lives! A terrible tragedy that the world should not forget. We certainly will not!

We wanted the best possible childhood memories for our children and the peace and safety of country life seemed preferable to the London rat race, so we bought a country home, Long River, aka 'The Shires'. It would be tougher on John, who would have to commute, but better in every other way; the schools nearby were good, the dogs and children would have the garden, there was lots of space, and there were nice thick walls between us and our neighbours. We also decided that now was the time for a full-time nanny, rather than an au pair. We were very lucky to find Sindy, who works a morning and afternoon split shift, with a break in the middle of the day. She is firm and kind and the children love her.

That is the short version of the story of 'How did we come to be?' Whatever the logistics, nature, within her blossom and beauty (with a little human intervention) has truly flourished...

We are often asked how we chose our children's names.

Our first set of twins, Amritsar and Tara, were born in Mumbai and our egg donor was an Indian woman; as a result, they are Anglo (Irish) Indian. In respect to the lineage we thought of the name Tara which in both Gaelic and Hindu means 'star' (and she really is our precious little Star).

The name Amritsar is, in fact, a place on the borders of India and Pakistan. You have probably heard of it as it's a very holy place for the Sikh religion. The most holy Golden Temple is at its heart. The word Amrit is actually a Hindu boys name and Amrit means 'food of the gods', a little like 'manna from heaven' (for God and the Israelites) so Amritsar is 'the place of Amrit'. And I have always thought it is a very beautiful name.

When it came to naming Thor, I was friendly with a gay couple from Norway who had just had a baby girl. One of the guys was called Törgeir, known as Tör, which I believe is a very popular name in Norway. I kind of liked the anglicised version Thor (aside from super heroes). In fact, I have met a few

5

people from Norway on my travels and each and every one of them have been great. John loved the name too. The God of Thunder - he certainly is.

Finally, we felt that Hebrew names would be appropriate with Aaliyah and Caleb as an Israeli agency helped with the surrogacy of our younger twins. Aaliyah means 'ascended' and Caleb is the word for 'faithful'. Both children were in fact born on the roof of the planet in the shadows of Mount Everest. The two names just seemed appropriate.

Chapter One

October

"What I really want to tell him is to pick up that baby of his and hold her tight, to set the moon on the edge of her crib and to hang her name up in the stars."
— Jodi Picoult, <u>My Sister's Keeper</u>

Well, why have I decided to do this and what do I want from it? Who are we and just what could I write about? Good questions to embrace at this early point...

Throughout the baby years I simply didn't have any time in the day for keeping a diary. Just the sheer exhaustion of it all left me drained, and that is with the committed help and support of John and the nannies. The feeds, the nappies, the crying, the sleepless nights... Not to mention the giggles, the 'aaah oooh's', and the running up the stairs with whomever sat on my shoulders, tiny hands grasping at my face, hanging on for dear life and screaming loud with the excitement of the moment! There really wasn't the inspiration to share what seemed a very precious time. But babies grow steadily, yes, all five of them. Now they are very much little people, and it seems that we all have so much more to say as we're all participating in our BIG family life.

On the day that I started my diary, the little ones were on the top floor, put down for an afternoon nap while our nanny, Sindy, had her midday break. I'd been sitting at my desk for a while when I realised there were noises and giggles coming from above. I went to the bottom of the stairs and called up to them to settle down. All was quiet for a short time, when again I heard giggles - and little feet running across the floor above my head!

This time I went upstairs, only to find they'd taken off their soiled nappies and managed to smear them over the tiles in the bathroom and all over Aaliyah's bed linen. Sindy arrived back at this point and she wasn't at all happy about the 'poo incident'. Teaching children the difference between right and wrong sometimes seems like it's going nowhere. But it will stick eventually. I know this because our two older twin girls are the best-behaved children ever – of all time EVER! Well most of the time, I guess...

I certainly don't want to sugar-coat this time in our lives – it is an uphill struggle a lot of the time; many days start with screams from the little ones and, indeed, finish with screams from the little ones.

Coming from London, I never saw the point of driving, and just jumped on the Tube or a bus if I needed to go anywhere. Throughout our years together, John has done all of the driving; he's had motorbikes and various cars, and we've ended up enjoying the luxury of a BMW X5 4 x 4. But when John found out the second set of twins were on their way he panicked and looked frantically for a seven-seater option. We now enjoy the delights of a Mitsubishi Shogun. Our nanny Sindy is on the insurance and fully accommodates the weekday school and preschool runs.

Every couple of weeks our babysitter Nikki comes over for the evening, which allows myself and John to go out for a meal, just the two of us, alone, with no children, no shrieking or sticky fingers – just the two of us! Bliss!

John passed on a conversation he had with Thor recently, after his wallet went missing:

John: 'Thor, have you been playing with my wallet, where are my credit cards?'

Thor: 'Daddy, I put them away, safe from the little ones!'

Daddy: 'Thor, you are one of the little ones!'

Thor: 'No Daddy, I'm big now.'

Daddy: 'So Thor, where did you put them?'

Thor: 'I can't remember, Daddy, but they are safe.'

We didn't realise when the names were considered that they would add up to the word ATTAC (Amritsar, Tara, Thor, Aaliyah and Caleb) with the order resulting from the timeline of the births. All of our children were born via a caesarean section so the weight of the babies determined who was the first born. And no, absolutely not! I don't care what anyone says - that's enough! There will be no sixth child with a name starting with the letter K...!

I guess not every small baby is assigned a 'baby name', well maybe not officially, but I'm sure that most little bundles of joy get called a myriad of cute-sounding nick-names, and no doubt a certain one will stick as the parents get accustomed to the sound of it.

Our children's baby names started with Tara. It was on a long car trip, driving from Candolim, a small town with wide and unspoiled beaches on the shores of the Arabian Sea, back to the raging, bustling, honking metropolis of Mumbai. We only stopped a couple of times during the thirteen-hour trip, and it was when we stopped for lunch that it happened.

As I walked from the car towards the food shack, holding Tara, I started making cooing noises to her, hoping to generate a giggle. 'Oooh oooh,' I was sounding, whilst holding

9

her close to my face and bouncing her gently. To my surprise and delight she replied 'Aaah oooh,' and I reactively said 'Boo boo.' Putting two sounds together constitutes a word as far as I'm concerned. And that was how Booboo was named!

Now we have twins, don't forget. If Tara got the 'oooh' in 'Aaah oooh', Amritsar had to have the 'aaah', so Amritsar became 'Baabaa'.

Thor, on the other hand, was quite the screamiest of babies; in hindsight, his name was obvious from the beginning. He would wail, crashing his clenched fists down loudly on the nearest surface. Are you thinking of Barney Rubble's son in the Flintstones? We were! So 'Bambam' was a clear winner as a baby name for Thor.

When it came to the youngest of the brood, I wasn't really planning on 'baby names,' but since we had gone down that route, I thought we should keep it in the same style as the other names. So, Bimbop, boopsnoop... only kidding! Haha. Beebee and Bobo were named. Caleb's name being shorter as he was our littlest one. A very calm and chilled out little baby, and when he was first born, he was the wrinkliest of all of our children. It kind of looked as if he was frowning with all the lines on his forehead, but he flattened out and no Botox was required...

So, there you go. Booboo, Baabaa, Bambam, Beebee and Bobo, our 'not so famous five'.

When Tara and Amritsar were just one year old, we had a brilliant au pair in London called Essie; back then she lovingly referred to Remus as Remo (something I picked up on) and I often call Gracie 'Grace Grace' as I do with 'Thor Thor' (it's a Thai thing)! Anyhow – one day I referred to Remus and Gracie as 'Remo and Grace Grace' and Aaliyah was clearly not happy.

'Their names are Remus and Gracie, Dadda,' she shouted, and started to get very upset.

'We all have baby names, don't we Bee Bee?' I insisted.

She thought for a moment and said 'Yes we do Andi,' (Thinking Andi was my baby name) and she giggled. Dadda had to smile.

A dark and windy October evening, children all in bed, found us settled cozily in front of the television. (Do people still call it that? Am I out of synch for not calling it the TV? And does it really matter?). Our dinner was a deliciously nostalgic meal of salads and charcuterie, reminiscent of our August holiday in Provence.

Yes, Provence was the children's successful introduction to the swimming pool, and we were all excited at the thought of them being able to swim and splash about in the water. There were lots of giggles and arm flapping in the excitement, ear-piercing shrieks and dancing on the spot, and it took all of our efforts to get armbands, flotation jackets and rubber rings on all five without one of them running off and tumbling into the pool. Eventually they were ready, and one by one we got them in to the water, John and I holding on to the little ones until they gained their confidence to float freely.

After a lot of screams and splashing, gulps of water, and coughing, all of them were doing the doggy paddle and gaining confidence by the minute. The first one to jump in with just her flotation jacket was Aaliyah. She is a very determined young lady and totally fearless. Thor of course saw an opportunity to 'covet' yet more stuff (he loves to covet things) so he promptly added her armbands to his, grabbed the watermelon rubber ring and got into the swimming pool, splashed about for a moment and then started screaming 'I'm sinking, I'm sinking...'

I'm really looking forward to the pool in Devon at half term.

The few days leading up to our Devon weekend break were chaotic. The children were beside themselves with excitement, and we were beginning to wonder if we were doing the right thing. We managed to get each of the bags packed at least three times, what with one child retrieving something from their case, and then another child following suit. Finally, impressing on them that they might not be able to go if their bags weren't packed and closed – and left closed! – they complied. The only thing missing were the swimming togs and armbands. We searched high and low; the children 'helped' by removing every item of clothing from their wardrobes and chest of drawers and dumping the lot in the middle of the bedroom floor, whereupon the dogs decided that the pile of clothes was a very comfy bed and settled down for a snooze! At least the children didn't unpack their holiday bags again! We finally decided that the missing swimming things must still be packed away in the eves, where we might have stashed them after our holiday on the Cote d'Azur, last summer. Sindy volunteered to go and search for them – alone - and the next morning disappeared up to the attic; she came down happy and victorious, waving the swimming bag in the air; this resulted in the children becoming over excited, dancing around and generally shrieking at the tops of their voices.

The provisions bag was packed and ready the day before we were to leave, including all of those things I said they would have to wait until they were at least seven years old to enjoy. At that point I had to laugh. We don't do sweets, but crisps and the dratted chocolate were unavoidable. They get given sweets in their party bags occasionally (from the multitude of birthday parties) and that is ample. It's like they have all grown up, weaned off of their diet of milk and on to juice and squash. I am happy now though as if they want a second drink at mealtimes, they are always given ice cold water. A thing they now actually even request.

The big day finally arrived, but before we could leave for the wilds of Devon the children were booked to have their flu vaccinations, and John had to finish the arduous job of mowing the lawn. Our friend Jo had picked up the keys earlier, so the dogs will be well cared for in our absence, and she would be calling in that night to give them their evening run, and thrice daily until our return on Monday. The dogs were getting excited as their dinnertime was around the corner.

By two o'clock that afternoon Sindy was transporting the little ones to the doctors for their flu vaccination and John had just finished mowing the lawn. With sweat on brow he made his way to the terrace. The grass was gilded green and shining with brilliance once more. Reminiscing on the autumn 'leaf fall', the ton of crispy leaves, brown and dull, had all but gone. Just a handful endured, hanging on to the branches for whatever little time remained for them. The sun was shining - and hot! In the shade of the bay window the thermometer read nineteen degrees, but in direct sunlight it felt like summer's embrace once again. I whipped off my tee shirt and a little sunbathing was had. The middle of October, who would have thought it!

At three o'clock John had gone to collect the girls from school and I was settling the little ones in the car. Thor was sleeping like a log and Aaliyah was snoring merrily in the middle. Caleb was awake and being very well behaved. He then told me that he wanted to wee, which was very good as we had both Thor and Aaliyah on potty training and thought

Caleb was maybe six months off. Aaliyah then woke up and started groaning and shouting. Five minutes later, with the arrival of John and the girls, her foul mood quickly dissipated. We were off!

Now, for those of you who have never had the pleasure of being trapped in a car with five small children on a long journey, here is a flavour of it. Four o'clock was still some way off when the dratted 'are we there yet?' raised its beleaguered head. My heart sank; we had a long drive ahead of us.

All was calm for a while, and I should've known it was too good to be true! Caleb started shouting and Thor was saying 'Be quiet Caleb, stop shouting'; that quickly changed to Thor shouting 'Caleb stop shouting.' Then I was shouting 'Thor and Caleb stop shouting'. The others were quiet for once, and John kept his eyes on the road. And when Thor said 'I see a small deer asleep beside the road. His leg was near the car. He was asleep,' I had to smile sadly at his innocence. A very observant little boy.

To the delight of the children A Bi-Plane appeared, swooped and circled above us, and there were lots of 'look Dadda,' and 'Daddy, can you see?' There was a fair bit of bickering going on in the back, which I ignored, but then we had to find a lay-by for Thor, Aaliyah and Tara to have a pee in the shrubs. Stonehenge was spotted in the distance, 'We're about halfway guys!' and we all got very excited, and then 'Tara pinched me,' came from the back seat.

'Stonehenge, Stonehenge is coming, look, look,' Amritsar was screaming and pointing. Aaliyah was more interested in the cows in the fields alongside however, and Thor was screaming about cow poo. Sonny and Cher came on the music system. We play a lot of 1960's music for the children. It just seems so much more appropriate in its innocence and optimism. Caleb was trying to sing 'I am a spaceman,' and Thor was shouting 'Caleb hit me, Caleb hit me'. They can't actually reach each other with Aaliyah sat happily in the middle!

Aaliyah was given a sticker at the library visit with preschool that morning, and she had stuck it on her belly button. 'Look Dadda, look,' she shouted at the top of her voice. Amritsar was giggling maniacally in the back seat and tickling Tara, then Aaliyah and Caleb started doing the same. Thor stared out of the window, totally uninterested.

And in amongst the pandemonium I spotted a car in a lay-by, toddlers in the back having a punch up, driver's door open, and a mother on her knees, cleaning off her car seat with wipes, and I thought 'There but for the grace of God, go I!' Cass Elliot just came on singing 'Own kind of music'. Respect!

Some of the rolling landscape either side of the road was a real treat for the eyes. Thor remarked about the long shadows and how it would soon be dark. Clever boy. Where did he learn that? Was it from me? There were several more cries of 'Are we nearly there yet?' in quick succession from Amritsar, then Thor and Aaliyah joined in.

John was bored of the music and wanted 'Music to Watch Girls By,' and I said 'If there are two rubbish songs in a row, can we change music again?' He wanted to know who was going to be the arbitrator, and as Thor was nodding his head I said, 'Thor can arbitrate,' and added 'Do you like this song Thor', and he replied 'Yes Dadda'. Hehehe.

'Look, Dadda, look!' Amritsar had spotted two paragliders floating past us in a nearby field, and all the children started bouncing and pointing. The next song was rubbish and we eagerly awaited the next song... 'Up, Up and Away in My Beautiful Balloon' started playing and Thor was asked whether he liked it... a resounding 'Yes!' But then again, we all secretly like it don't we?

'Sheep, sheep, sheep,' was all I heard then and guessed we had just passed a flock of sheep. Caleb had been clutching the nappy-change bag for the entire trip and kept opening the zipper. It seemed he couldn't close it and kept screaming 'Dadda, Dadda. Help!' I was getting a neck ache with turning around so much. Out of sympathy, Thor and I allowed John his fix of Andy Williams as 'Music to Watch Girls By' was playing.

The sun was preparing to set in front of us. A magnificent display of mottled cloud and the sun's exhausted rays beset us, as did Gene Pitney. I started screaming 'Are we there yet'? Thor pulled a handful of Aaliyah's hair from her scalp, and she was screaming and kicking about something completely unrelated. We saw a Llama in the midst of a field of sheep – did it get any more surreal? Tara was shouting 'Hello Llama, Hello Llama.' Because of heavy traffic the car was at a standstill beside the Llama and they were all shouting 'Hello Llama.' We could see a statue of Buddha in the sheep and Llama field!!! And then I found half a bag of wipes at Caleb's feet, pulled from the packet. He was no longer the nappy-bag monitor. Naughty Caleb! The half term traffic sucked. Usually things sped up once past Stonehenge - but it had been a constant crawl for the last two hours. Thor and I gave the thumbs down for the next song playing, and I wondered if we would be swapping musical genres again? Thanks Bobby Rydell. Though Tara started singing - or was it whining? - in tune to the song! How very theatrical of her! The Mavericks were a compromise for us, but the children decided they all wanted 'Shake, Baby, Shake,' by Lush. We were trying to teach them the art of compromise - they could have their song next.

The traffic had improved vastly as we began hitting 70mph. Were we legal? We were going with the flow however! I don't drive but I sympathise with those behind the wheel. We were as slow as a tortoise for so long and then running with the hare... I spoke too soon. We were back walking with the tortoise. But the children got to see a 'Blue Tractor' on the opposite side of the road. The sun was almost much set by then and the moon was shining on my left-hand side. It would be full in a few days; I hoped it wouldn't be cloudy on Monday so we could see it clearly!!!

Oh dear, Thor said he could smell something strange! 'Is it coffee?' Aaliyah asked. 'What is it, what is it?' she started screaming. Thor looked at her calmly. 'You don't need to worry Aaliyah.' Thor then added, sounding strangely sinister, 'The moon is following us Aaliyah,' and they all gazed at the silver moon in awed silence. It was dark by then and I had resorted to Google maps for directions.

We arrived to a warm welcome and the gracious hospitality of Alistair and Lorna; their two dogs, tails wagging, also greeted us at the main farmhouse door. Aaliyah smiled and gave them the biggest hugs. Their two cats fled and hid, and that was the last we saw of them. John went with Alistair to purchase the six biggest portions of fish and chips I have ever seen. Dinner was a big hit, washed down with copious amounts of blackcurrant squash and white wine. You can work out who drank what! The 'Thatched Barn,' where we were sleeping, was warm and cosy. Surprisingly all five settled quickly, though it was almost three hours past their normal bed-time.

We had been invited over to the farmhouse for breakfast, so after a sound night's sleep, we headed across the yard in the bright morning sunshine. A light dusting of oil on the 'eggy bread' and wafer-thin crepes, cooked on the range, made the open kitchen a little smoky, but this soon cleared and everyone ate vast amounts; it was delicious.

We ventured out to the local seaside town of Seaton. The weather was unusually sunny and warm, with only a mild breeze. Our first stop was at The Seaton Tramway, and we knew that the Seaton to Colyton old-fashioned tram-ride would be a big success with the children. It was, and caused great excitement whenever the driver blew the tram's whistle. It's difficult to know if the tram ride, or the choosing of a toy each in the gift shop, was more exciting!

We progressed on to the actual seafront. It is not such a commercial one, just a rank of houses, a few businesses and a shingle beach. Ice creams were purchased from a small hut on the road beside the beach; it seemed to take ages as each child chose what they wanted, then decided they wanted what someone else had chosen, and so on. We decided to eat them in the car, something Aaliyah wasn't happy with. Needless to say, we had our first major meltdown of the day, followed by Caleb becoming angry and throwing his ice cream on the floor of the car. Thor, Amritsar and Tara finished ice creams calmly and asked for tissue to clean off. 'I want to be good; I want to be good,' Aaliyah screamed, but there was no sign of her anger calming until we were nearly back at the holiday home. Lunch was a simple matter of toasted bagels. There was excitement and shouting again as we prepared for our 4.30 p.m. slot at the pool.

We swam and squealed and splashed happily in the outside pool for well in excess of an hour. Remember that this was the latter part of October in the UK and it should have been too cold to swim! Once showered and back in our civvies, we were invited up to 'the big house' where the not so famous five enjoyed olives and little bear corn puffs, followed by spaghetti Bolognese, all finished off with home-made chocolate brownies. We so appreciated Alistair and Lorna providing such a fantastic meal for them; they ate the lot, and we took them back to the 'Thatched Barn' and put them to bed where, within minutes, they were all sound asleep.

Our hosts arrived fifteen minutes later to serve us a well-prepared paella made from chicken stock made with chicken legs, and roasted garlic and vegetables. It was spectacular, served with large prawns and scallops; a very well-engineered, gastric delight! We used to summer in Spain when John's mum and sister owned an apartment there many years back; it was near Marbella on the Costa del Sol. We ate paella a lot and I can, with hand on heart say that our host's version far exceeded anything that we had previously savored. Thank you, thank you. And to top it off, we couldn't get over how good the weather had been!

The next morning Alistair and Lorna bundled their two dogs into the car and we followed them on the twenty-five-minute drive to Sidmouth. We parked, crossed the road and walked down to the pebble and sand beach, to the west of the town center. The beach is flanked at the rear by enormous, red sandstone cliffs. Jurassic in age, this coastline is well known by fossil hunters and happy, beach-going tourist alike. The dogs loved it, the children loved it, we all loved it. The further along the beach we walked, the more confident the children were to embracing the water's edge. The waves weren't particularly big to begin with, but they were on the tidal side of high. The beach was slowly getting smaller and smaller and the children were running into the water more frequently, flapping and laughing, splashing each other, splashing us and the dogs! They were all soaked through within fifteen minutes of arrival, absolutely wringing wet; they were shoeless and topless by the time we'd been there for twenty minutes. At thirty minutes we had to give up on that beach and walked along the coastal path to the second beach. I must admit, though, that we forgot to bring towels. A big mistake, but with the sun shining and the temperature in the early twenties, they all dried off fairly quickly.

The next beach was closer to the town. The sun was hot and there wasn't a cloud in the sky. We may have forgotten the towels but we hadn't forgotten the buckets and spades, and enjoyed a further two hours of sand castle making, climbing the granite boulders (to the rear of the beach) and just having a good time in general.

Once back at the holiday house, de-sanded and showered, I was thinking back to the last time we were on the beach. It was this summer in the South of France. The children were all in swimming costumes and armbands; the beach was a little more glamourous than Sidmouth perhaps, and the warm Mediterranean waters were Azure blue and very inviting. We all loved the pool at the villa, they were in for a couple of hours each day and I am so glad everyone now has the confidence to just get in and start splashing around. Though being fully clothed in Sidmouth, maybe they had a little bit too much confidence! Note to self: 'Always bring towels!'

The final night away was a whirlwind of thanking our hosts over a Pinot Noir and a chilled Chardonnay. My food offering was a Roast Pork and bacon joint, pigs in blankets, lard roast potatoes, glazed carrots, butter-sautéed Savoy cabbage, fine green beans and a jus (gravy) made with pork stock and the juices from the meat!

We were woken the next morning by Amritsar tapping Sidmouth pebbles together at 6.15 a.m., and the bedroom invasion happened at 6.45 a.m.. Another breakfast at the farmhouse of 'eggy bread' and crepes, then a mass cleanup before we said our goodbyes at 10.30 a.m.

The journey back was smooth. 'Are we there yet' only resonated a handful of times, there were no toilet stops and the children slept for seventy percent of the trip. A far cry from our outward journey. The dogs went crazy on our return and we were soon settled and very much at home again.

The phenomena of Jam Making in my life started soon after moving to The Shires. But even before that I had attempted blackberry jam and, to my dismay, I was rubbish at it. Three times I re boiled the stewed fruit, and that is after bottling and sterilising the jam jars thrice, and all I had was blackberry syrup. It was a total disaster and I felt like giving up, but I am rather glad that I stuck with it.

This past year, with a more than competent nanny and the children either at school or preschool, I had a lot more time on my hands than I used to. As babies, there wasn't really a free moment to spare from dawn till dusk (and then some more) and I only found the time to start 'The Art of Preserves' as a hobby during very rare, spare moments.

The stuff is as pure as sunlight. I don't have a particularly sweet tooth, but I confess, real Jam is COOL, and consists only of pure fruit and sugar. If you brought some from the shops (naughty you), check the label for ingredients and if there is anything other than fruit, sugar and citric acid in there,

I would bin it. Harsh this might sound, but here's a thought: you could very easily make your own!

I recently made five jars of one of my yummy combo jams. I don't think I've mentioned the flavour combos before, so I'll fill you in; the last combo was 'Kiwi and Lime'. Totally amazing on hot toast, dripping with butter. Some more of 'Dadda's Jams' combos are: Rasmelon Berry, Peach Peary, Black Grapple, Ginger & Pumpkin, Strawlime Berry and Blue Cherry Berry. Just a few amazing combos alongside the usual classic flavors, but like pumpkin, you can 'Jam' with just about any fruit (or squash).

It would seem that 'Dadda's Jams' have gone savory this month. The glass jars of ruby red relish with little flecks of mustard seed peeking through the glass have been thoroughly sterilised, labelled, and stacked beside the spiced pumpkin jam that was made over the weekend. I decided to see if I could make something akin to 'Branston Pickle,' and after googling the recipe and tweaking it, as I always do, there is now a tasty new chutney to add to the 'Dadda's Jams and Pickles' range. If you should decide to give it a go, chopping all the vegetables in the food processor makes light work of it.

The apple crop was poor this year and most of the apples we had from our orchard I have used as my source of pectin in 'Dadda's Jammin'. A trade secret I am happy to share: none of my well-set jams contain any shop purchased pectin. Sorry 'Certo'!

All jam makers know that the latest project needs to be immersed in boiling water for at least fifteen minutes to insure it will stay perfect for the upcoming year (or two) in the cupboard. I'm still not won over by 'Nigella's' just turning them upside down for a few minutes.

'Dadda's Jams' are definitely a massive hit with the children, plus family and friends know exactly what they're getting for Christmas.

'Jam is funky' and everybody loves it...

Chapter Two
November

"The moon made me do it."
— Unknown

I had been a cigarette smoker since my youth, and finally decided I needed to quit; I had tried half-heartedly a few times over the years, but this time I meant it. I knew in my heart that John didn't like it, even though he hadn't said very much on the subject. It was a bad example for the children, although I usually didn't let them see me smoking, and it was bad for my health - I didn't need a doctor to tell me that! I was trying to cut down as a prelude to giving up in the New Year, and had swapped some time ago from actual cigarettes to an e-cigarette.

My e-cigarette has a small battery charger that is generally plugged into a socket above the dish washer. On this day, whilst emptying said dishwasher, I could see there were a couple of chickpeas sitting in the filter and I bent to retrieve them. Behind the filter I noticed a black wire; at first, I was mystified, but then realised that my e-cigarette charger had been placed into the dishwasher at some earlier point. Drat! Knowing that this incident would have been one of the little ones, I called them all into the kitchen. Standing shoulder to shoulder, and with a little fancy footwork, they jostled and nudged each other before becoming still and looking at me to see what I wanted of them.

'Well,' I asked, 'who put the charger into the dishwasher?'

Caleb, the quietest of the three (mostly), piped up 'It was Thor.'

'Thor,' I said, 'was it you?'

'No, Dadda, it was Aaliyah,'

I looked at Aaliyah and raised my eyebrows.

'It was Caleb!' said Aaliyah, pointing at her twin.

Rather than having one little liar, we clearly had two, if not three little liars. I had all three of them standing around the open door of the dishwasher, looking innocent but somehow managing to glare at their siblings at the same time!

I wagged my finger and looked at them sternly. 'I'm going to leave you to think about it. I'm going to leave you for just one minute, and when I come back, I want you to tell me the truth.'

We all know that children are rubbish at keeping secrets, so I knew the truth would raise its head sooner or later. I went back after a minute and both Thor and Aaliyah pointed accusingly at Caleb. He was looking at his feet, shoulders sagging, silently consumed with whatever emotion it is that three-year-old's have; was it guilt? Anger at being found out? Or indeed anger at the other two for ratting him out? I picked him up and placed him under my left arm (gently of course) and marched him up the two flights of stairs to bed.

All of the little ones usually scream and shout when they've been so naughty that they are banished to their bedroom, but on that occasion, there wasn't even a murmur from Caleb, which was highly unusual. Half an hour later I looked up to see if he was okay only to find him fast asleep, and I decided to let him stay there until lunchtime. I wondered if he might be coming down with something, but he seemed his usual self when I brought him down for lunch.

Thor makes me smile as, on the odd occasion when he has been naughty, he will look me straight in the eye and say 'Naughty Dadda, Naughty Dadda.'

A last thought on Aaliyah's moments of extreme naughtiness, and she has had quite a few! Of late, her behavior has improved significantly, and it's all down to the thought of going to Naughty School. You see, we have an imaginary local school for naughty children! It is simply called 'Naughty School', and it's run by 'Mrs Snodgrass'. She is a no-nonsense woman in her late fifties; in my imagination she dresses in clothes that would indicate she has time-travelled from the year 1954! Perhaps a green tweed, two-piece suit, horn rimmed glasses that hang from a chain around her neck when she's not using them, and a tight grey perm. Let's just say that the threat of going to Naughty School is our plan B with Aaliyah. We all need a plan 'B' don't we?

After a lot of thought and discussion, John and I decided to celebrate both Halloween and Guy Fawkes during the weekend between the two dates; we planned a bonfire party followed by a little trick or treat hunt with two of the neighbouring families. And 'Hallo-Fawkes Weekend' was born! It's all so fusion nowadays isn't it?

Costumes would, of course, be needed, and I had a chance to get to the shop's midweek. I had my orders! Amritsar wanted to be a witch and I was thrilled to find a black cobweb dress that would do the trick. Tara, on the other hand, wanted to be a Vampire, and the scarlet wench's dress that I found was absolutely perfect. Thor was determined to wear the bright orange pumpkin costume that we already had at home, and Aaliyah and Caleb wanted to dress as witch's cats. I wondered if Amritsar the witch would be bossing the two little cats around all evening!

In preparation for our big 'trick or treat' hunt with our neighbours, the Tesco delivery included zero-sugar fizzy drinks, iced ring donuts with sprinkles, and a multitude of sugary sweets and chews. You've got to show willing, I guess, but I've never amassed such a stash of sugary things for the children ever before. The fizzy drinks were the diet variety however, so a few brownie points earned. Just the sight of the laden table, almost bowed under the weight of sweets and snacks, had the children running rings around the kitchen and shrieking in anticipation. With all that sugar I definitely don't think it will be easy to get them into bed after the party...

When I was young – I never thought I'd hear myself say that! – we made a 'guy' (for Guy Fawkes night) from an old pair of trousers strapped to a sweatshirt of sorts (anything with long sleeves) and the whole lot was stuffed with scrunched up newspapers. We used an old pillowcase filled with dead leaves for the head, and a hat was fastened on with one of grandma's knitting needles. A kind of introduction to taxidermy really! We'd take it out in the streets, in an old pushchair or buggy if we could lay our hands on one, and chant 'Penny for the Guy' to any passing adult, holding our hands out in the hopes that coins would be dropped into them.

Anyhow, I think my childhood was the initial fusion of our British Bonfire night, and our American cousins 'Trick-or-Treat' celebration on All Hallows Eve. So, sod stuffing your old sweatshirt with newspapers and asking strangers for fifty pence, and bring on stuffing your pockets with sweets and as much cash as possible, conned out of the friendly and ever so slightly mystified neighbours in surrounding streets. All very different now of course.

On the day, the children donned various costumes. As usual, the best laid plans went awry, and after much foot-stamping, swapping of clothes, cries and giggles, Amritsar was still enjoying her witch look, complete with broomstick, Tara had rejected the scarlet vampire dress in favour of a very round orange pumpkin costume, Thor looked very fetching in a vampire cape and false pointy teeth, and Caleb was another, smaller, orange pumpkin to match Tara's. Aaliyah was wearing a cute little black cat outfit, home-made from luminous spotty tights, a long-sleeved tee shirt, and a shop bought cat mask and tail. Much to their dismay I made them home-made potato wedges with hotdogs, so they at least had something decent in their little tummies, before diving into all the sugary treats that would be on offer later on.

Excitement was mounting; they watched as Daddy began 'weaponising' long pieces of bamboo into harpoons, ready for the marshmallows later, but they looked rather dangerous and I was most definitely the 'bad guy' when I insisted they couldn't run around the house chasing each other and the dogs with them, and to leave them outside ready for later. Then we had hours of what sounded like 'are we there yet?' as the not so famous five asked in whiney voices 'where are they?', 'when are they coming?' and 'where are the sweets?' The sweets were, of course, in the kitchen, hiding in an antique wardrobe known as the housekeeper's cupboard.

I was still slaving over a hot stove. For the adults my chapatti dough was transformed into twelve lightly floured balls; later I would roll each one out thinly, before cooking for a minute or so, and serving up with the curry. I say 'curry', but it had escalated to four curries, Channa, pea curry (mutter), chicken curry and a lamb curry. Each with a slightly altered spice mix. The spicy smells in the kitchen were quite heady and mouth-watering, but I would wait until tonight before tucking in.

We had invited all of our neighbours for the 'Hallo-Fawkes' party; seven of them declined, all retirees, and pretty much done with 'good will to all'. Children were only acceptable within their own families, and their grandchildren were the only infants that were tolerable.

The neighbours who joined the event all had children; it was dark when they arrived and we drank Prosecco and then lit the tiki torches. The children jumped up and down, wanting lit torches too, but we thought that might just be asking for trouble, so torches ablaze, avoiding the bats that were franticly swirling above our heads (yes, we have a local bat population), we left through the back door, headed to the bottom of the garden, over the lane, into the woods, across a stream, and to the designated bonfire area.

Once the bonfire was lit, all of the children gazed in wonder as it caught and crackled and flamed, and they 'oooh'd and 'aaah'd and pointed at sparks leaping upwards into the night sky. John's harpoons were soon made safe by me snapping off the sharp points, and marshmallows were just squashed on to the ends of the bamboo rods. All of the children enjoyed toasting (supervised I might add!) and chomping on the marshmallows, and drank their fill of hot chocolate from the two large thermos flasks.

All six adults did a great job stopping the potentially fatal stab wounds, pokes in the eyes, falling into the blazing bonfire and general possible mishaps, in the darkened (though tiki torch-lit) wooded environment post nightfall. On our return, I went into overdrive to set up the kiddies' meals, and then the finale of twelve hand rolled chapattis, rice, and the four carefully constructed curries for us grown-ups to enjoy.

While the excited children were eating at the kitchen table, John hid the sugary treats around the hallway and a couple of the downstairs rooms, and once everyone was seated and calm, we handed over little empty bags for the children to fill as they hunted and found the 'treasure'.

'Ok children. Are you ready? You'll only find treasure in the living room, the dining room, and the hallway. Don't go upstairs! And not in the kitchen or bathroom! Thor! What did I just say? Stay downstairs. Aaliyah, leave Gracie! No, she doesn't eat sweets. Here Gracie. Come here. That's it, good girl. Caleb! Out of the kitchen! Right, are you all clear? Good. Off you go!' I clapped my hands, and watched as they frantically ran from one room to the other, not really looking properly until Amritsar squealed that she'd found something. They all descended on the one area and, pushing and shoving and squealing, and now and again trying to take things from each other's bags, they did a more thorough sweep of the downstairs, finally calming down when their bags were full and John declared that they'd finally found everything there was to find.

The adults chatted and drank wine for another half an hour while the treasure hunters examined their finds and tucked in. It was quite late when the neighbours left, waving and smiling, with calls of 'thank you' ringing in the crisp November air.

What a day! We were all exhausted, but everyone thoroughly enjoyed it and I think we will probably do it again next year! Maybe!

With the sweets that were consumed, I have to say, I didn't once have to ask for a 'please' or 'thank you'. If only that were the case with the more mundane actions, like being given a drink or their dinner. To be honest, our oldest two are mostly model children. There is the occasional prompt for a please or a thank you, but usually they are very polite.

The hounds are very food focused and at the whiff of a treat they get quite excited and either sit in front of me or, in Remus's case, start to spin. He will spin and spin and spin until finally, when the treat is in my outstretched hand I loudly say 'Gentle' and he'll take it. He can be a bit of a snatcher with food, so if he tries to snatch it, I hold onto the treat and repeat, 'Gentle' until he complies. Gracie nibbles the treat with tender care.

Thor will deliver a very cheery and sincere 'thank you', but only if you hold on to whatever it is he wants to thank you for until he has actually thanked you - very much like Remus! Yes, you've guessed, there is the occasional tussle, but it is usually me who wins! The same can be said of Aaliyah and Caleb.

On another subject, I was getting bored with the quality of beef mince available in the supermarkets; for an edible sauce, the beef needed up to three hours cooking time in order to tenderise! Firstly, whilst frying the meat gently, the sheer volume of water that the meat releases essentially steams it, and then the amount of fat the beef exudes over the extended cooking time, well, it's shocking! Thankfully we've always got plenty of kitchen roll to absorb what collects on the top of the sauce. I noticed in France a much more tender cut used for minced beef for Bolognese sauces, producing perfect Bolognese in thirty minutes. I finally came to the conclusion here at home to just use pork mince (with a similar cooking time) and lots of garlic. Perfection is reached and we all eat very well.

It was while staying in India, Thailand, and Nepal, that I perfected my culinary love and enjoyment of Indian and Thai food. When I was researching how to make 'Channa' I Googled it, looked at a few recipes and thought 'that'll do.' I half forgot half of the three recipes I had looked at and cobbled the remainder of the information back together in my head, and there we have it, Dadda's own take on the perfect chickpea curry.

So, here's Dadda's Channa recipe! No method necessary, you don't even need to fry the onions, so an oil free curry it is. Remember you have to soak the chickpeas overnight, then boil them for an hour or two the next day. Mind you, you'll have to skim the chickpea water when it reaches boiling point. Or, for an easy life, just open a couple of tins. Use as many or as much chickpea and onions as you like, tinned tomatoes or just tomato purée, and some diced red or green capsicum peppers. The spices you can play with. An easy option in India is to just buy a Channa masala spice blend, but that's not necessary. Recently I have used fresh garlic, ginger and chili (the holy trinity of spices), though the dried versions would be perfectly acceptable. The next two spices are also essential and they are cumin and dried coriander. Turmeric is much loved in India but can overpower in flavor and colour, so go careful with it. If you've used tomato purée, great as this gives a great colour combined with the turmeric. You could chuck in some Garam masala if you fancy, but I don't feel the need. Add salt to taste, and I recommend plenty as food needs to be tasted if you are planning on enjoying it! Spice needs to 'cook out' it's raw taste, so during the next hour or so, taste a teaspoon-full of the liquid every now and then. After the hour or two's cooking time, crush a single chickpea between your fingers (cool it down first of course) and if it's cooked, you'll know. Now with a potato masher - mash to your hearts content. I like mine quite puréed but with the occasional chickpea to bite on. Heaven on a plate, served with steaming rice or chapatti. I prefer the latter for a more authentic taste of the Sub Continent.

Everyone should have the competence to cook a basic food such as rice. My method will guarantee a perfect result, so please heed the very basic steps that follow.

Don't use the hob - remember the last overcooked rice dish you made and now want to avoid? Use your microwave – please! It's really good for a couple of things and rice is one of them. Don't use the usual big brands of long grain - easy cook blah de blah. Just buy regular basmati rice. Use a ceramic or Pyrex dish with a lid. I always place two sheets of kitchen towel on the revolving plate within the microwave in case of some spillage. Fill your dish with a little under 40% of dry rice. Over 50% will be a big problem. Fill the rice-filled dish with water and leave to soak for fifteen minutes. Swish with your fingers and tip the water out, then cover again with cold water. Swish, empty and fill again with hot water. Don't weigh it, just fill with water that looks about twice the height of the presoaked rice, and add a good amount of salt. Cover with a lid, or a plate to seal, and microwave the hell out of it for fourteen, maybe seventeen minutes, depending on being 750 or 850 wattage. After said time, remove with oven gloves and turn out onto a roasting tray or large dish. It will look like a block of solid rice. Don't be fooled! Use a fork and gently break apart the clumps to move them away from the central mass, and kind of break up into smaller grains with the fork. Perfect cooked rice, never over-cooked or under-cooked, always flakey grains of perfectly cooked, quality rice. Cook as much as your dish will allow.

Use maybe half for your meal and spoon the remaining half into a freezer bag. Seal, and once cold, use your fingers to break up any remaining clumps of rice, and freeze. Your next rice meal will be as simple as a defrost and a three-minute microwave and it will produce a second, even simpler dish of perfect, flaky rice that is cooked to perfection. Our latest special fried rice was indeed a case of defrosting a frozen bag of pre-cooked basmati rice. Too easily achieved and such an astounding result. Bon Appetite!

This month I'm making some sweet candies to give away for free at the girl's school Christmas Fayre. Yes, I could have just purchased a ton of fun-size delicacies, but I opted to make my own sweets, starting with orangettes made with candied clementine dipped in chocolate. My very favorite sweet in the whole wide world – ever! I think they will go down better with the parents, so I am making home-made pastilles for the little ones. It is, in fact, the parents that I want to impress as I have taken this year off from Elfing, yes, I said Elfing and I am taking a stall for the occasion and selling gift boxes of 'Dadda's Jam' as well, and we'll see how that goes.

I made a large quantity of clementine orangettes and left them to dry out on greaseproof paper. Once fully dry, I gave them a dusting of castor sugar and popped them into an airtight tin, ready to be dipped in chocolate. I also managed to prepare some chocolate truffles, and the apple and orange pastilles are ready to be chopped up and chocolate coated when the time is right. All done with the hope of selling a jar or two of Dadda's Jams at the Christmas Fayre. I imagine all the thought and preparation won't be worth it financially, but I don't really care as I'm feeling a strong Christmas vibe at this point, and giving without expecting recompense is making me feel like I'm part of humanity and that life is not only about the take.

I must tell you that I tested the sweets out on the children, just to check they were ok, and I was blown away by their reactions. Tara said that I am a 'magician' with sweets, Amritsar shouted out "best sweets ever!' and Caleb's eyes just rolled back! Although it's been a labour to come up with the various pastilles, candied fruits and chocolates, I've enjoyed spending my time on the project, and all of the girl's classmates are looking forward to the home-made sweets at 'Dadda's Jams' stall at the Fayre.

Chapter Three
December

Brightly shone the moon that night
Though the frost was cruel
-John Mason Neale

There was a bit of a skirmish in the kitchen one Sunday evening! All afternoon while I was slaving over a hot stove and making a roast pork dinner, Remus and Gracie were getting under my feet and wanting scraps. While we ate, they prowled around the table like wild animals circling prey; the meal was delicious - even if I do say so myself! - and by the time we'd eaten our fill there was very little left. The children must have been extra hungry because they ate everything they were given and ended up with clean plates. Subsequently, the roasting tin that we usually put down for the dogs to share and lick, had very little left in it. I almost didn't put it down for them, thinking that it didn't seem worthwhile, but they were begging, as they do in the kitchen, and getting excited, practically jumping up to get at it, so I placed it on the ground for them to share.

I think Remus tried his luck and began to nudge Gracie away, his head was in the pan and he was pushing her aside with his body. She gave a low throaty growl in warning; Remus nudged her even further away, but she was having none of it and gave a sharp bark, then snapped at him. Although he is the top dog, she sometimes tries to assert herself over him. On this occasion she was successful and Remus ran off, tail between his legs. Actually, I think he'd had most of whatever was left in the pan by then anyway. They either ignored each other or sat at opposite ends of the sofa for the rest of the evening. Very emotional creatures, dogs, but 'falling out' over the licks from the roasting pan? Crazy! I thought they would cheer up soon enough and things would get back to normal.

However, the following day the mood was a rather sombre one and they were still sitting at either end of the sofa. Some of the looks I could see as they accidentally caught each other's eye – really, if looks could kill! After the scuffle in the kitchen the previous night they were still avoiding each other like the plague. It took another day before they began to thaw towards one another, slowly and shyly, and that evening, children asleep (I hoped!) I finally sat down beside the rapscallion pair; Gracie was nestling on Remus's hip. A good sign that they were friends again after their quarrel.

I spent a couple of nights in London in order to do some of the Christmas shopping; we had most of the presents already, but I wanted to find something special for each of the not so famous five. Madness you might think, going into the capital at the busiest time of the year, but you just can't beat the atmosphere; pubs were heaving with happy merrymakers, Christmas music blared out of every shop I passed, twinkling lights were everywhere I turned, and the range of things one can buy is mind boggling! I lived in London my entire adult life, and love it there.

Sindy had previously booked a couple of days off too, to do her own Christmas shopping in London, which meant that John had the children to himself. He coped admirably, and absolutely loved it – except that is, apart from the bit where Caleb removed his nappy and smeared the reeking contents around his bed, teddies, toys, books, face, and hands! John wasn't best pleased when he found the mess but apparently all Caleb did was laugh!

Christmas shopping was fun, and trying to find special gifts to match the emerging identities of the children was a really enjoyable challenge. They are like real little people now instead of babies, becoming tangible personalities with foibles and charms, the beautiful light side - and occasional dark side - to their characters developing. I had to think about them carefully before choosing what to get for them.

Amritsar works hard at whatever she turns her hand to; she is good at art, considers colour and form, and combines different characters in a thoughtful way when it comes to drawing. She is our Little Miss Sunshine, with a beaming smile, especially when she is on the school stage at the 'achiever's assembly', waiting to collect one of the special blue certificates. She's an excellent reader, proud of her achievements, thoughtful, loving, and affectionate, and for a girl of five, I am in awe.

Tara is the perfect name for our Little Star; she does like to take to the stage, so maybe a Star she will turn out to be. She is quite happy grabbing a microphone and singing and dancing with emotion; indeed, many of her school achievement certificates are for movement and dance, as well as counting. She can lead in many conversations, and is passionate, caring, independent, and calm; she shows empathy and exudes kindness. She has a very strong bond with Caleb, the littlest of our family, as she takes him under her wing and looks out for him. Everyone loves her dearly.

None of us slept well through Thor's baby years as he was so loud and screamy; then the terrible twos gradually merged into the not-quite-so-terrible threes. I think a lot of it was simply down to him wanting to communicate so much. The women at his new preschool all doted on him, and even back then he was practicing his 'charm initiative'; he is a very unique little boy. Just being able to talk changed him so much. It was not just his step forward to communication, but from a very early age he started to form opinions and ask questions. He talks a lot now, and there are still the occasional moments when he finds that he has to shout, but he's primarily gentle, caring and considerate. He won't go to bed without his 'Kiss and Hug'. Mind you, he can get quite moody if things don't go his way, or there's something he wants that he can't have. Thor 'The Coveter' totally likes to 'covet' things, he covets everything and anything, whatever he can find will do; he collects bits of paper, cardboard, blankets, whatever is portable and he can get his hands on. And he has his beloved MiMi, his very best bear that goes everywhere with him. He is a very loving little boy and often says things out of the blue like 'I really like you Dadda' and sometimes, just sometimes, I get a 'I love you Dadda'. The heart melts...

Now Aaliyah and Caleb share the same timeline, though they have advanced through it at slightly different speeds, and they are still quite little. They were model babies, unlike Thor, had lots of sleep and four-hourly feeds to begin with. Aaliyah was a bit louder than Caleb when she yelped for a feed or over the discomfort of a soiled nappy. Most babies are predictable and you're lucky if you get a smile or a giggle, but Aaliyah did giggle lots and, being very close to Thor in age, it seemed like it was him she was trying to catch up with, leaving poor little Caleb behind somewhat. She crawled before Caleb, stood before him, and even made her first faltering steps way before. She is a very strong-minded little girl, sometimes pushy, and I think her determination will lead her wisely – watch this space for updates! She is really happy and full of life; she has a lot of potential with her character as it is, but there is a belligerent side, the one we have to keep in check with the thought of 'Mrs Snodgrass's Naughty School'.

Caleb, as a toddler, got there eventually. He crawled, or rather, dragged himself at first. He developed later than the others as Aaliyah did it all six months before our Calo (one of his nicknames). Eventually the dragging turned into a fully propelled crawl with his bum in the air. He was a bit rubbish with balance, so standing and walking came late also. Back then he was a quiet little boy and he didn't communicate well, quite the opposite of Aaliyah. But big sister Tara stepped in at a very early point and did all she could to protect and encourage him. I remember his first three steps, and his sense of accomplishment was a joy to behold. So, he is a boy who is a little laid back but, with encouragement, he gets there in the end. There's nothing wrong with being a late developer, and once you have caught up you might just even surpass the rest! He has only just started to form sentences, which is great as he will start proper school next September, and there's lots of time to practice before then. He is more screamy now too. It's like he was silenced for a long period and now he is finding his voice and sounding more legible, he really wants us to know his wants and even his frustrations.

I must just tell you, there was one thing that Caleb got first though and that was the hair. Masses of curly, silver blond hair. He's had it cut, but it's still fairly long. Aaliyah's hair has taken ages to grow, but there is some length there now and it's beginning to resemble Caleb's curls. So now it is fitting that Aaliyah is reunited with her twin brother Caleb as they look more like the twins they actually are nowadays. Thor doesn't mind at all, as there's only room for one little bolt of thunder in our house.

On the afternoon that I got back, laden with parcels and bags, John and I were like ships that pass in the night! Just enough time for a quick hello and an update, and he was heading into London for his work Christmas party at a North African belly-dancing restaurant! He is sure to be exhausted on his return!

The School Christmas Fayre was great fun. I went along just before it opened to set up my stall to sell Dadda's Jams and Chutneys, and I took along all the sweets I made last month. I had a banner printed, to stand behind my stall, and it read, 'Dadda's Jam' and beneath it, 'Transcend Your Day' and that's just what something like a home-made jam can do...

The school hall was festooned with Christmas decorations, and a large tree was sparkling in the corner with flashing lights and dozens of baubles. There were numerous stalls selling all sorts, cakes, lucky dips, sweets, and little home-made gifts and toys, and several tombola and raffle type stands. There were Christmas carols playing in the background, and a Santa Clause had his grotto in one of the classrooms, with little gifts for the children. It got crowded pretty quickly, and the noise level swiftly turned into a racket. The not so famous five appeared at my stall halfway through the evening, buzzing with excitement. They'd each won little presents at the tombola stall, and showed me handsomely decorated cupcakes that John said they were allowed to eat after their breakfast the next morning. I'd sold thirty jars of Dadda's jams, and I was delighted that the home-made candied fruits and pastilles went down a storm. The headmistress very kindly purchased three jams for a tenner, two of them being the rather boozy spiced pear, raisin and rum, the last-minute X-rated Xmas Jam. Not to be squandered on the children please - and if eaten with chocolate, very likely to blow you away...

The ride home was noisy to say the least. Although Tara and Amritsar were singing loudly, Aaliyah was fairly quiet. Caleb was nice and chilled, and Thor was noisily voicing his opinions. It wasn't until everyone poured out of the car that we realised why Aaliyah had been so silent; her raffle prize pens had been silently marking just about every inch of skin on her body! She looked like the Tattooed Lady in a Victorian Circus! Oh dear – her bath was a very long soak and a scrub to see if any of her original self remained!

Like many of you probably do, we decorated our living room with Yuletide garlands, positively radiating the spirit of Christmas, and we had purchased a twelve-foot conifer to stand in the big bay window next to the piano. After the fight to get it into the house and firmly wedged into the four-pronged Christmas tree stand, and the battle to get it standing straight without getting my eye poked out, I stood back to admire the shape and height of it. It actually touched the ceiling, and it was perfect! And once it had its sprinkle of fairy dust (lights and baubles) it would look magical.

Usually I collect foliage from the woods to make some of the garlands and wreaths, but I just didn't have the time this year, so while the children were still at school and preschool, Sindy and I took some of the lower branches off of the tree to make conifer wreaths, adorned with red satin bows. Sindy took hers home for her front door, and mine was hung on ours.

The following day I completed decorating the tree whilst listening to a Christmas CD, and my mind became a swirl of nostalgia. All those memories of little red glitter balls, and spiny glitter stars, brought for John's and my first Christmas together all those years ago. But what did we accumulate along the way? China ones with the children's baby hand prints. Baked glitter stars from the girls' first year at big school. Papier Mache bells and hand-painted animal globes, a mass of felt baubles and little rabbits from Nepal. Little Thai Elephants on a string, sea shell wreaths from Hawaii. Each one a memory of a time in our lives. I had been so lost in thought that before I knew it, I'd nearly finished!

Once the tree was decorated to my satisfaction, I then boxed and wrapped four trios of Dadda's Jam, Christmas presents for the girls' teachers. For the Head mistress, a handmade chocolate box containing twelve chocolate dipped orangettes, as she had requested a few freebies when she purchased the X-rated Xmas Jams at the Christmas Fayre.

It sucks to have a birthday so close to Christmas, and Thor's was on the 22nd. We hired the village hall and booked a magician to entertain the twenty or so children and their parents that had been invited to celebrate his fourth birthday. Four is a good age, and his sense of reason has come on a lot in recent months. Mind you, there's not been a day as yet that hasn't involved at least one major breakdown! Beware the might of Thor!

The big day flew by, much as a fast train does when whizzing through a station and not stopping there. Remembering the events is a bit of a blur, partially down to the mulled wine, but primarily due to the constant din of not just five children, but rather twenty-five. Sindy and her sister Sally were great! From midday until two o'clock, they made sandwiches and stuffed yellow cardboard lunch boxes with ham and jam sandwiches, pombears, mini sausages, miniature tomatoes and a Cadbury's chocolate roll. I made plenty of mulled wine to offer to the parents attending the party and I think it went down rather well; the adults were getting merrier as the afternoon sped by.

The village Hall was decked with Minion balloons and tablecloths. The theme, Thor's favorite ever, was crowned off with a Minion Birthday cake, and he was proudly wearing his new Minion jacket. The magician was great and entertained the mass of both children and adults alike. It was over far too quickly, and before we knew it the hall was empty and Sindy and Sally waved us goodbye while we, two tired dads, loaded our car with five very tired children, two large bags of gifts, and four bin-liners of party leftovers sorted into general waste and recyclable. The day was a huge success, and we only had one or two little 'outbursts' from our not so famous five. Thor was given a Minion 3D puzzle globe, which Daddy, Amritsar, and Tara, all pieced together for him and they were all jubilant when it was finally complete.

Christmas was as chaotic as you'd expect and a week-long weekend it did seem. We had the usual bed invasion at about 6 a.m. and the children were overexcited, bouncing and screaming and wanting to see if Santa had been. We persuaded them to have some breakfast first, and then let them loose into the living room. Tara and Amritsar dished out the presents, since they could read the names on the gift tags, and it was a matter of the little ones ripping off the paper, seeing what the present was, and then jiggling up and down and wanting the next present. John and I took over giving out the presents, so that the girls could open some of their own gifts, and managed to finally give out the last one. Once they knew there was nothing more forthcoming, and with some encouraging words from Daddy and Dadda, they started investigating what they had, wading through discarded wrapping paper to check out each other's presents as well. There were some traditional carols playing through the 'Hey' Google smart speaker and John and I each had a cup of tea while we watched them. It was wonderful that they were each old enough to appreciate Christmas, and their happy innocent little faces will stay with me for a long time.

This year our pigs in blankets were actually chickens in blankets - don't tell anyone. Our turkey actually had a name, Kelly (bronze) and the bird arrived with exact cooking instructions plus a thermometer and a box of Malden sea salt. After the present-opening, I made a start on the dinner while John supervised the children getting washed and dressed, and then we all collected the discarded wrapping paper. We made a game of it – I held the black bin bag open while the children scrunched up the paper and lobbed it into the bag from a distance. I did help by trying to catch it with the bag, and we were soon down to just the presents - toys, books, new gloves and pyjamas, slippers, jigsaw puzzles, you name it - littering the floor and tables.

We got all of the children to (sort of) help to set the table, and when our Christmas dinner was ready, we all sat around the very festive-looking table, pulled Christmas crackers and donned the coloured paper hats that spilled out of them. Funnily enough it was quite an orderly affair and we all ate well; I think we are at a point that the experience of a roast meat dinner is a lot less stressful than in the past. The turkey was delicious, but far too large for us and, temporarily, I wrapped up all the leftovers and stored them in the fridge. Too full to move in any kind of energetic way, we retired to the living room and switched on the television.

The children had the attention span of newts and went, within minutes, from playing with one of their presents, to watching and shouting out answers to 'Team Umizoomi' on Netflix, to terrorising Daddy, who was trying to play Candy Crush on his iPad - and then doing it all over again. During Christmas Day and Boxing Day we watched 'Chitty Chitty Bang Bang', which the children loved (they hated it last year), 'Charlie and the Chocolate Factory', and 'The Wizard of Oz'; for us grownups 'The Holiday', 'New Year's Eve', 'It's a Wonderful Life' and, most recently, 'Love Actually'. Once the children were in bed and settled, we enjoyed the BBC's new rendition of 'Poirot' - isn't John Malkovich a rare talent?

There were many outbreaks from Thor and Aaliyah after so much excitement, and Mrs. Snodgrass was even called on the telephone one night as Aaliyah was so badly behaved. Her school for 'Naughty Children' was threatened, and Aaliyah promised she really wanted to be a good girl and was given a few days to prove that she could, indeed, be a good girl. Naughty School's new term started on the Monday and Aaliyah was told that she would have to pack a bag as the school is a boarding school. Aaliyah tried very hard after that to behave. Don't forget, Naughty school is just a fiction and used every now and then to steer Aaliyah on the right path. Thor, on the other hand, was still a bit too ballistic to comprehend 'Naughty School' and its implications. We just had to rely on the threat of the 'Thinking Chair' or bed as the ultimate threat, and luckily these seemed to do the trick.

One small 'Q & A': What did I do with the rest of Kelly the turkey and the ham joint? Well, we continued to feast on it (Kelly) and the large joint of ham with a second 'Mock Roasty' on Boxing Day, and then it was all wrapped up and put into the freezer, as it won't last until New Year's Day. Nestled in beside the frozen turkey gravy and the last of the blanched sprouts!

Carrots don't freeze well, so we'll steam and glaze them on the day.

On the evening of Boxing Day, I was quietly stacking the empty toy and gift boxes outside the back door when all of the not so famous five spilled out into the darkness, wearing jimjams and slippers; Thor was clutching the string and weight of his still inflated gold number '4' balloon from his birthday. The Twelve Days of Christmas started sounding out of the open door, and suddenly, without warning, we had an impromptu sing song and a dance. It was freezing out there, so as we all sang and danced in a circle, 'Five go-old rings...' I managed to dance them all inside again, still singing. Inside it was warm, the fire was crackling in the grate, the dogs were curled up beside John on the sofa, and the children and I danced and sang. That was what it was all about!

This year's cutest moment had to be on the Friday before Christmas coming home from having had dinner with a friend, Lizz Nelson, in Wimbledon. Every house that was externally adorned with Christmas lights was duly commented on from the back seat by Caleb. A softly spoken 'Kimmah Ligh' would resonate every time we passed a festively Illuminated building. Every few minutes that passed, 'Kimmah Ligh', 'Kimmah Ligh', 'Kimmah Ligh'. In the end we were all playing the game, not just Caleb. So now I think of 'Kimmah Ligh' and smile to myself.

Many moons ago, as a young man, I pondered on 'What must I know to improve myself in life,' and qualifying as a chef was at the top of the list. I did so, back in the day when being a celebrity chef was not really an option as a career, and since then I have chosen to eat well in life and share the outcomes with the people I care for! Catering-wise, I ended up in catering management and that was the end of being an underpaid, overworked idiot. I gave up being a chef a lifetime or two ago in favor of design - designing clothing, accessories and jewelry, even though my degree was actually in silversmithing! But I still take great pride and enjoyment from creating tasty wholesome food for my friends and family.

Fact: I have not served boiled carrots throughout my entire adult life. I have to share something with you: stop cooking carrots if you aren't open to the idea of glazing them! They taste like crap if they are simply boiled or steamed, and eating vegetables should not be a chore. I used to follow the traditional recipe for Glazed Carrots but bugger that! Just steam them until soft but still with a bite. Stop them cooking by drenching with cold water from the tap. Once chilled, put them in a bowl and in the fridge. Now, just before service, in a frying pan, a slug of stock or water, a pinch of salt, teaspoon of sugar and a knob of butter - melt and reduce until a syrupy consistency is reached, then toss your chilled carrots in the syrup until hot, steamy and glazed. Delicious, tasty and a big goodbye to boring old boiled carrots, which will now be a thing of the past.

Why go with cold cuts and pickles when a 'Mock Roasty' is so quick and easy to do? Deep fry some cooked, peeled potatoes (microwaved is fine), glaze the precooked carrots as above, heat pre-blanched vegetables in the microwave (blanched green beans, cauliflower or whatever). Peas are easily cooked from frozen. Slice the meat cold and reheat in the gravy. Voila! 'Mock Roasty!'

Save the cold cuts for the 27th as we did. Turkey breast, gammon ham, cheddar, Stilton, Branston (or home-made pickle), cornichons/gherkins, baby beets and buttered baguette, the only word for it is 'Wow'!

We are all faced with the 'turkey leftovers' dilemma each year, and for the fact that on Christmas Day, I immediately froze the two turkey legs, simply because that way, you get to choose what to do with them at a later date. Don't make that mistake and try your hand at making a turkey curry with the brown meat. After some thought I realised that my regular meatball recipe, slightly tweaked, was perfect. Just make sure you roll the meatballs as small as a chocolate truffle.

So, our family dinner on New Year's Eve ended up being spaghetti and meatballs using 50% pork and 50% finely diced brown turkey meat – it was sublime. Only breadcrumbs, fresh herbs and seasoning added. The taste, as opposed to using pork alone, was amplified and I didn't even think I was consuming turkey leftovers as the texture was soft and tender. Another WOW! Time well spent and practice makes perfect. Job well done!

Please reassess turkey leftovers and consider meatballs (or meatloaf) as a real option. Maybe next year at least.

Chapter Four
January

*"Wisdom of the Ages: Do the aliens on the moon pull down their pants and 'earth'
their friends for fun? ▢"*
— Matthew Heines

I didn't want to preach to you about New Year resolutions as, to be quite honest, I didn't make any this year. That is unless I mention that we've all got room for improvement, don't we? And that is something that we should be working on constantly throughout each and every day, year on year, throughout our lives.

We've returned the boxes of Christmas decorations to the cupboard at the top of the stairs where they live for the rest of the year. It was very easy to open that cupboard door, and I've had to fix a bolt, quite high up, to stop little hands pulling the boxes out and distributing the contents through the house! Yes – that's the voice of experience! After removing the decorations, the living room looked less ornate and back to its familiar, comforting warmth; The carpet was temporarily cleared of trip hazards and vacuumed, the huge pine cones were removed from the mantelpiece, all surfaces were cleaned and polished, and the tree was lying outside on the terrace. Everything was back to normal.

After all the excitement of Thor's birthday, his party, the Christmas Fayre, and Christmas itself, the girls were back to school, and the little ones were at preschool. Just before Christmas we learned that the preschool the little ones attended for four days a week was suffering financially and might not make it through this coming term. Amanda, the head, informed us of this just two days before the Christmas break, saying that she was going to jump the sinking ship! I guess the reduction in wages may have been her ultimate reason for going, but the three remaining staff members left 'holding the fort' are in potentially volatile times and we wish them luck. So, our little ones continue their daily routine with a slight change - we have found another preschool for them that operates from 9 a.m. until 3 p.m., much in line with regular schooling, and every Thursday they stay for the whole day. Which means that every Thursday I really do get the day off!

On that first Thursday I had invited a friend, Richard (a local artist) over for an early lunch; we hadn't met up for a while and it was great catching up over a simple meal of salad, cheeses, and crusty bread. The dogs circled the table, stopping at each of us in turn and checking the floor under our chairs as we ate, waiting for scraps. They were gratifyingly pleased to get some leftovers in their bowls, and then we escaped them, the crazy hounds, and went out to a local town, Hungerford. John's birthday was the following Tuesday and I wanted to search for a couple of birthday gifts for him.

It was one of those crisp sunny afternoons, and it was fun browsing in first one, and then the next, antique shop; they were all grouped at one end of the High Street, with a couple more at the other end of town just past the string of boutiques, pubs, and florists, and the bridge over the canal. I felt liberated to be out without any children hopping around my legs or screaming at me, just wandering along in a very civilised fashion with another adult! And then immediately felt guilty! I love them all desperately and wouldn't be without them, but just now and again, very, very occasionally...

That same evening after the children were in bed and John and I settled down to some quiet time, Thor called for Daddy. It sounded, in John's words, 'terribly urgent' and he jumped up and ran the two flights of stairs to see what Thor needed. Five minutes later he was back, and threw himself onto the sofa beside me. 'Water! He wanted a glass of water!' We had just settled back down with a glass of wine each, when Thor started shouting again. John jumped to his feet.

I tried to stop him. 'Thor doesn't need anything; he's just trying it on. Let him scream it out for a while or he'll have you jumping through hoops!'

'How can you be so cold? Listen to him!', and he was gone again, up the two flights of stairs. He was back minutes later, mumbling something about a book and MiMi.

I shook my head and handed him his wine. I was determined not to say 'I told you so' and less than five minutes later Thor was shouting for him again. This time John got up calmly and climbed the stairs in a measured pace instead of rushing. He was gone for some minutes and I thought I could hear his raised voice echoing down from up above. When he came back down, he flung himself on the sofa again and crossed his arms. 'This is exhausting! I'm not going up again just to entertain Thor and his various whims!' I was very good! I handed him his wine without a word, and slowly sipped mine, trying to hide a little smile that I was struggling to keep under control. He was getting no sympathy from me!

If you're a parent, you'll know how the children will play you, pushing as far as they can while they test boundaries, and you just have to try to out-maneuver them. I know there is a certain wisdom to being four years old (so Thor imagines) and in having the upper hand, but come on! Parenthood can be exhausting; if you let them triumph time after time, you're setting yourself up for despair. Just something to ponder on...

The Sunday before John's birthday we had a Mock Chicken Roasty; the children loved it. It seemed that things were getting much better at the dinner table, and their slightly improved table manners might have had something to do with letting them have a slice of the home-made birthday cake that I had baked to celebrate Daddy's birthday. It was a masterpiece, ring shaped, iced, and covered in 'hundreds and thousands!' We saved the second half for the next day, Monday. For John's actual birthday on Tuesday Sindy had agreed to a sleepover with the children so that John and I could go out and celebrate.

John and I met up in the West End after he finished work; I love going to the West End, it's always buzzing, and there are people of every nationality spilling out of pubs and restaurants onto the pavements, smoking and chatting and generally milling around. It's especially vibrant at night when theatre and restaurant lights are lit, people are dressed up going to or coming from the theatre, and there's always music and laughter. I like that!

We had a table booked at J Sheeky's and it was looking particularly cheerful and welcoming with its red awnings, glossy red paintwork, and golden sign letters, all shining and shimmering in the street lights. The outside tables were full, despite the chill in the air, but the table we had booked was inside. The food was truly impeccable, and after taking our time – it's a rare occasion that we are alone in London and we made the most of it! - we arrived back to the London flat for John to open his birthday presents.

The children had all signed a card that the little ones made at preschool (we've stopped producing cards from each and every one of them if it's not necessary), then we enjoyed some white wine while John examined his presents. 'What were the presents?' you might ask. Well, with the price of robotic vacuum cleaners having dropped sufficiently, there was one of those (it even self-docks to power up and there is a mop function!). A pair of Apple wireless ear buds, four antique silver napkin rings and a large, bone handled magnifying glass with matching letter opener. My afternoon browsing the antique shops in Hungerford had paid off!

Thor was extremely naughty at preschool. The all-day one he attends on a Thursday almost called to ask us to bring him home! Luckily, they did not, but they did let us know about his screaming and shouting and generally behaving like Bambam when Sindy arrived to collect him. They allowed him to continue until 3 p.m., but to almost be excluded from preschool? Come on Thor, you gotta buck up to the challenges of life and do some growing up! You know, up to that point there had never once been a day without some shouting and screaming about something. Not a single day without some major incident happening. I kept telling him that he was four years old and he had to settle down a little, but he didn't like to listen to anything and tended to pretend he hadn't heard me, let alone analyse what was being asked of him. He was shouting a lot more, mostly talking sense, but he always had to talk as loudly as he possibly could! The iPad (kindle fire) he got for his birthday had hardly been looked at.

On the other hand, Aaliyah had, by and large, been well behaved (no biting or screaming) and was given Amritsar's old tablet; she asked for it more often and happily engaged with the (educational) games with relatively little assistance from Amritsar. She could happily play on it for extended periods, concentrating hard and working out how to solve the puzzles, with Gracie curled up on the sofa beside her. Good for her for figuring things out for herself.

Caleb had recently been spilling his drink at the dinner table; we don't know why, but at every meal, without fail, Caleb seemed to be knocking over his cup. Just a phase, we hoped. His diction was slowly improving, although there was still long way to go before he was up to speed. No 'poop' incidents either, but never say never! He tried to communicate 'potty' a few times as well, which was brilliant! He got the idea of what he was meant to do, but just sat there and, if there was a small pee-pee from Aaliyah or Thor (that we hadn't flushed immediately) sitting in the pot, he tried to claim it as his own. He's a chancer, and no mistake! But I knew better! Thor and Aaliyah seldom have an accident now which is great. Though occasionally screamy and badly behaved, they are definitely on course for big school in September.

Amritsar and Tara have both enrolled in extracurricular activities on Wednesdays after school, and this term they have chosen different pursuits! Tara (being our very own little 'performer' and possibly a future actress?) joined in 'Film Club'; Amritsar enrolled in 'Craft Club' as she loved being arty and a little crafty too (in the nicest possible way). She had been persevering with sequin art since Christmas, small pins and sequins you have to pin to a picture of sea animals. It's very complex, even for an adult, and she was doing really well. They both also made Paw Patrol bead characters that needed ironing to fix the beads together. Oh, my goodness! Tara asked me to iron her Marshall the Dalmatian character for her, but before I knew what was happening the dratted thing smudged and squished into a multicoloured smear; she was very upset with me, to say the least. I did help her to remake it, but we asked Sindy to do the ironing part, just to be on the safe side! Sindy did iron it, but very, very cautiously!

Our old nannies, unbeknownst to me, started using metal utensils when they were cooking in my precious copper pans that I had purchased in France a couple of years back and had completely and utterly ruined them! I could have cried when I realised what they had done! I recently had them re-tinned and afterwards they looked brand new, so shiny and sparkly that I am not sure I will ever use them again! (I was tempted to send the old nannies the extortionate invoice for re-tinning them!) Anyway, I wasn't going to take them out of the box until John had put a shelf up for them, and then they can sit there all twinkling and polished and I can gaze fondly at them. I tried not to badger him, because he knew what I wanted, but he spent quite a bit of time sitting on the terrace contemplating putting the shelf up. One day...!

It was a Wednesday when our nanny Sindy went off for her midday break and Aaliyah, Caleb, and Thor, were upstairs having an after-lunch snooze. All was calm and quiet and I wallowed in the temporary peacefulness. Just moments after Sindy returned I heard her telling the little ones, in her no-nonsense voice, to 'sit on the sofa' whilst she surveyed the destruction that surrounded Amritsar and Tara's bunk beds! They had all sorts of 'bits and bobs' stowed away in various special shoe boxes and music boxes, but the little ones had strewn them all to the winds, emptied the contents onto the bedroom floor and scattered them everywhere, and all they could do was scream and shout at Sindy; the concept of guilt was not in any way present!

They descended the stairs, having been told that they would make right the damage when Tara and Amritsar returned from school, and I scowled at them as sternly as I could! Thor and Caleb just giggled, though Aaliyah screamed that she was sorry. 'I want to be a good girl; I want to be a good girl,' she screamed, throwing herself onto the sofa headfirst and kicking her legs.

I listened to the shrieks and giggles for a moment and finally said loudly, in a very firm tone, 'Enough is enough!' The little ones quietened for a moment and then watched as I picked up my phone and made a few finger motions.

'Am I speaking to Mrs. Snodgrass?' I asked. 'Yes, it's me again. This time they really have gone too far and they do not feel at all sorry - is there a chance that Aaliyah, Caleb and Thor can begin 'Naughty School' on Monday morning'?

'What? They can?' I said, 'Perfect. We will finalise things on Sunday. Thank you very much. Goodbye.'

'No, not Mrs. Snodgrass, no, no, no!' screamed Aaliyah. Thor added 'No Dadda, no' and Caleb just looked on shamefaced. Anyhow, Sindy went off to collect the girls and things were later tidied up, but the little ones were desperate not to go to Naughty School and their behavior improved somewhat, even if just temporarily. Hence, they by and large tried to be better behaved for the rest of the week, but can a leopard change its spots? Humph, me thinks not! But remember that they are only three and four years old, so this whole fiction is basically the ultimate deterrent. There were some ups (with such well-behaved children) and a few downs, where they have all pushed or hit or screamed at each other (I decided that biting had finally been eradicated). I guess that these three things were only ever directed at each other and not us, their parents; it was a good thing as it showed that they did have certain limitations. So, it wasn't too bad really. They were all commended after their Sunday evening bath for (overall) being so well behaved, and I faked a phone call to

Mrs. Snodgrass saying that we did not need to start 'Naughty School' after all. They were very happy and all went off to bed smiling.

Doing the math on this one, I can truly say that, with the girls sixth birthday coming up in March, I have pretty much had a cold for the last three years. They started preschool three years ago and that's when this cold began. You know the way that children suck and chew on just about all of their toys and share them around with their fellow preschool attendees? Well, even with the girls at big school and the fact that they are more akin to washing hands and not sharing small plastic objects coated in bacteria with everyone, we still have the three little ones doing just that!

I wash my hands at least forty times daily. I scrub the kitchen table at least twice and to be honest, although I don't get stomach problems, I guess cold viruses are just too virulent. One cold follows on after another and so on. Looking at most of the old photos of our guys when they were preschool age, almost all of them have runny noses. Thor seems to be the worst, it's just one cold after another. Recently his nose has just been a snot factory and when it runs, sometimes it almost reaches his chin if unnoticed for even twenty minutes. It is only during the month of August that everyone seems to be healthy and without a cold. I am hoping that with them all at big school in September, the sheer volume of this will quieten down to a trickle. I really hope so. I'm tired of coughing and sneezing and blowing my nose and gingerly swallowing into the sore throat. Roll on September.

I make a vast array of quick and simple soups, and I think we did an asparagus, and a potato and watercress, in recent weeks. My favorite has to be pea and ham. Just the four ingredients really. Pea, ham, potato (don't bother peeling) and onion, plus a couple of stock cubes, water and seasoning (there's zero fat and loads of protein and fiber) I never liquidise this one, just pummel with a potato masher when the ingredients seem to be tender. Always check again for seasoning before serving. Best served with buttered baguette, or a cheese sandwich. Yum!

Victoria Plum Jam

Okay Victoria (Coughlan), this one's for you! The most basic recipe for jam is plum jam. It is the easiest and quite simply, one of the best jams ever! The darkness of the outcome is dependent on the ripeness of the plums. Two punnets end up being about 700g after you have halved them and removed the pits. Put them into a pan (no water), and put several splashes of pre squeezed lemon juice from a bottle. Gently bring up the temperature, stirring occasionally.

You want the fruit to steam down to a pulp.

When your mixture looks a little stewed add 700g sugar. Please note: NO pectin is needed for plum jam as plums are naturally very high in pectin. Cook on for another ten minutes. Your jam will become glossier and more translucent.

Skim the top to remove any of the scum that forms as and when. When it starts to look a little more gelatinous, after maybe ten more minutes, you will find it falls from a wooden spoon less rapidly. It will kind of hold together a little. Ensure you do not cook (in total) for more than thirty minutes. If you do the jam will take on a heavy, jammy taste that is not so good. You don't want to overcook your sweet nectar. This is the time to remove any remaining, whitish scum from the top

I always use a jam funnel, but as long as you go slowly and carefully with the kitchen ladle so that there are no spills on the rim of the jar etc, you should be okay. Please note that the jam jars, lids, ladle and funnel have all just come out of the dishwasher, so they are completely sterilised. This said, do be careful not to touch anywhere other than the outside of the jars and lids. Fill with the jam to several millimetres below the top of the jar and screw on the lid tightly. You may want to use a tea towel as the jar will be hot. Now place the jam jars in the biggest pan you possess and cover with water. Boil the jars for twenty minutes to finalise the sterilisation. I think that Nigella doesn't do this, rather she will just tip the hot jam jars upside down. This kills any potential bacteria below the lid. I opt for the traditional method however. If you don't have a pan big enough, fair enough, do it Nigella's way.

Hey presto you have a real treat ahead. The children will love it, but you might just want to keep it for the grownups, mixed with a small splash of water and drizzled over Greek yoghurt or ice cream.

Chapter Five
February

"I moon bathed diligently, as others sunbathe."
— Denise Levertov

Friends 'Glen and Victoria' (Jeary) were planning to tie the knot at the end of the month; Victoria had already had her Hen weekend, and Glen was holding his Stag do a couple of weekends afterwards. He'd opted for a boy's boozy weekend at... wait for it... Weston Super Mare, on the Costa del Zummerzet in the West Country. A three-night *'Incider!'* themed weekend at the Pontins holiday camp. 'What did that entail?' you might well ask! Well, to be honest, 'What happens in Weston, stays in Weston!' I think that only fair. I was planning on not staying for the last night as I always miss the children like crazy, and hoped to be home by 4 p.m. on Sunday. Sadly, I was going to miss the fancy-dress party (finale), but I was hoping there would be a few photos of the crew! Someone always makes a fool of themselves, so I was looking forward to a good laugh when I saw them. At least it wouldn't be me!

On the way to the Stag do I had arranged to see a very good friend, Sarah, who used to live in Bristol but had moved to Weston Super Mare; it had been ages since we last got to spend any time together. I was actually hoping that we could have got her an armband so that she could be an honorary 'Stag' for the weekend events, although I know that would never be allowed! I don't think she would have enjoyed it anyway, to be honest; I knew the bar was going to be very well stocked and reasonably priced, and I guessed there would be some comatose cider drinkers needing paramedic assistance before the end of the weekend. There would also be some crazy plan to play a prank on Glen!

Anyway, Sarah met me at the station, and we talked and talked and supped away on the finest champagne! We always seem to just carry on from where we left off last time we met; she doesn't realise just how great her company is and we talked on into the night, reminiscing, and laughing and giggling like teenagers! It was freezing that weekend, and a lot of the country had received a blanket of snow. The following morning, after leaving Sarah to make my way to the holiday camp, I slipped on a patch of ice and twisted my ankle. Drat! It was incredibly painful! There was no choice really, because I could barely put my weight on it, so I limped to the station and bought another ticket to get me home.

Sorry lads! I missed out on a weekend of alcoholic oblivion in favour of going back to The Shires, and did I get any sympathy for my poor swollen ankle when I got there? I think not!

The snow had fallen some six inches and the garden looked like a beautiful winter landscape from a Christmas card; I took a taxi from the station and arrived back in the middle of a fierce snowball fight with the neighbours and their families; it really looked like fun, and I was sad that I couldn't join in, despite the not so famous five calling and shouting at me to help them. After several battles between the families I believe that our crew won, overall. Good for them!

There was no snowman, which I had fully expected to see. Indeed, I was hoping for one that was a bit of an improvement on last year's poor soul! He had been only about two-foot-tall, with quite a large carrot for a nose, two wonky eyes made of stones and a black piece of wood – I was never sure if it was a mouth or a bow tie! Yes, that was Thor's handywork! The not so famous five were probably too busy with their snowball fights, and I could see that the sleigh had been out and well used, so it seemed that they had had a lot of fun in the snow while I'd been away. I discovered that actually, there had been a snow day the day before so the children hadn't been to school, and John hadn't gone to work as he was snowed in – four to six inches he said – and had worked from home. As adults, we have to hark back to what a snowfall here in the UK meant when we were children. A magical thing completely.

After the neighbours had left, the children and I spent a happy hour or so shelling monkey nuts to fill the bird feeder, which was hanging empty on the wisteria on the terrace. All five children worked really hard and we were hoping that the birds would enjoy eating them as the snow was still deep. No little worms for them to dig up on the lawn in this weather. We all felt warm and fuzzy after doing our bit for the birds and settled down to watch a dinosaur movie; we were cuddled up on the sofa with the dogs, the wood fire crackled and radiated heat on that most wintery of Saturday afternoons, and we could smell the delicious Moroccan shoulder of lamb that John was cooking in the kitchen. Perfect!

Later on, I saw that the birds had discovered the newly filled feeder. I even spied one of our resident robins having a peck at the supersized peanuts contained therein. Shamefully I admit that the feeder had not been filled since the squirrels vandalised it last year, in their vain attempts to gorge on the contents. Naughty squirrels, as they get to feast on the majority of seeds and kernels of the many trees and oaks in the general vicinity. I guess desperate times call for desperate measures.

After the weekend the six inches of snow had dissolved to almost nothing. As quickly as it had fallen, it had gone, and it left a patchwork of green and white lawn on which the squirrels played. Remus wandered out of the house and suddenly he spotted the squirrels; he froze for a split second and stared at them, then sprinted down to the bottom of the garden with Gracie hot on his heels, forever hopeful of catching one, but the squirrels sped up the nearest tree and left the dogs below, front paws on the tree trunk and barking up at the ones that got away. You've got to smile as there's never a victory for poor Remus or Gracie, and I doubt there ever will be when it comes to speedy squirrels, but they are persistently optimistic.

It was the night before the full moon; given the cloudless skies above The Shires I spent twenty minutes taking time to admire its luminous glow. Here in the crystal clarity of the countryside, with the lack of artificial light, the garden was illuminated with a frenzy of sparkles that was dreamlike in its luster. The woodland beyond took on a magical, almost fairylike feel. If you are ever entrapped by the glare and hubbub of the city, find a quiet place and moon-bathe for a few moments. It can be very meditative and grounding, which is always good for the soul, and you can find me here on clear moonlit nights doing just that.

My first birthday card had an Irish postmark, which meant it was from Granny and Grandad in Dublin; so, thank you, Hazel and Michael. My birthday was on a Friday this year and John and I headed into London – he wanted to take me out for a surprise meal. Well, the fact that we were in London and going out for a meal wasn't a surprise, but the restaurant we were going to was. As you know, I love London, and Friday nights always feel celebratory there, what with the end of the working week (for most) and anticipation of the weekend.

Everywhere was heaving when we left the flat; if I had to commute daily in the crowds it would be a very unpleasant grind, but since it was only now and again that I had to face it, it was bearable. We grabbed a number 9 bus and headed for the Aldwych, and by the time we stopped on The Strand I guessed that it had to be The Savoy we were dining at. What a special treat! Thank you, John! I absolutely loved it! While we were away, Tara, Aaliyah, and Amritsar, helped Sindy to bake a birthday cake for me. It was incredibly colourful, sort of round, and a little wonky, but all the tastier for it! We had it on Sunday afternoon and it really was delicious.

John's birthday gift to me was exactly what I asked him for - to pay for a chippie to come and rebuild a chunky mahogany coffee table for me. This coffee table was another rip-off purchase that I made on eBay, and it fell to bits in a flash! I splashed out two hundred pounds on this 'antique' table that turned out to be rubbish! It was basically four cut-down snooker table legs that were badly screwed into a mahogany top. It was an attempt by some antique dealers to botch together something from bits they had lying around, but don't get me going! Some of the rubbish available on eBay is scandalous! It looked great in the photographs, but there you go, enough said!

I really miss our old brass-topped coffee table; it was large and circular, with a hole in the middle. It was handmade, Indian style, with brass rivets in it (Victorian arts and crafts). The only problem was that the edges of the brass started lifting up from the wood, and became a bit of a health and safety issue with the children. Luckily, we were spared any sliced fingers - it really had to go, but it did look well in the living room. Safety above style sadly. I remember when auntie Sara's two were little, she padded every surface with foam pipe cladding and removed everything from the living room. Come to think of it, the room still looks kind of empty, even today! I do get it, but I have so many memories of our old brass coffee table involving all of our children. They used it as a house, a castle, a car, even a flying saucer. Plus, we stashed the sea of toys inside of it at the end of each day. I am a lot happier that we no longer do toys in the living room, it's good to feel like an adult again. But getting rid of our useful brass coffee table is, I guess, just one of the sacrifices we all make in the early years.

As you know, I'm a bit of a foodie, but I'm not by any means a restaurant or food critic. My birthday two years ago led to a major disappointment when we went to the Michelin starred Vineyard Restaurant not too far away. I had ordered a very 'blue' fillet of lamb, and the chef chose to substitute it with saddle. Saddle! The toughness of 'rump' really doesn't lend itself to being served almost raw! I did make a complaint and in fairness they didn't charge for my main course as compensation, but it was untouched, excusing the three mouthfuls of meat. Leaving in haste as we did, the bill still came to two hundred pounds as there was zero understanding of just how our celebratory meal was a complete wash out! I had but eaten a rather wispy smoked salmon starter and a few mouthfuls of inedible meat, and obviously Johns enjoyment of the celebration had been marred, so we decided to just not eat there again. But there we were, almost two years later, and had a very pleasant meal, though portion-wise, a little meagre. The carbs were nonexistent, that is if one did not include the two portions of very tasty home-made bread rolls that were served. The final bill was astronomical and made us reconsider things. And to be honest, the atmosphere was not sufficient to compel us to rush back. Front of house service was very good, but sadly the menu was lacking in that 'something dynamic' you would expect with a restaurant prizing itself on such a high level of quality, and which says that you are *'guaranteed to enjoy a very special gastronomic experience'*.

What with all that had been going on, I forgot to mention our first visit from the tooth fairy! Our crew went for a walk in the woods with Sindy; they had brought supplies because, as they had all insisted, going on a long walk meant that they might get very hungry! And as they had walked for some time, provisions were dispensed on the way home in the guise of chocolate hobnobs, you know - to restore energy levels and all of that! Amritsar's bottom front left tooth had been loose for around a week, so we were expecting the inevitability of a visit from the tooth fairy. Anyhow, the chocolate hobnob was enough to release said tooth from Amritsar's mouth, but sadly we were not there for the actual moment of the loss of the tooth. When they got back, we stared in awe of the little space at the bottom of her jaw.

Now isn't there a saying that for every door that closes, a window opens? And for sure there was! Personally, I don't remember, as a little fella, a lot about the process of losing teeth in favour of a second set, but just behind the hole that has replaced Amritsar's lost baby tooth is a very pronounced 'Big Tooth', that she will live with from this day hence...

John did a grand job sneaking upstairs to replace the tooth under the pillow with a shiny, one-pound coin! To be honest, I think she was expecting more, what with inflation. But we are going to have many, many more visits from the tooth fairy over the next few years of course, so they will have to accept that one pound is sufficient and we will have to perfect our stealth abilities, won't we?

And just as a matter of interest, have you ever seen an x-ray of a child's mouth? There are two complete sets of teeth in there! And truly, the mouth of a child is an astonishing thing to behold! Google it!

I had walked through the kitchen earlier and breathed in the very heady aroma of Thai yellow curry with chicken. I had taken the time to skin and de-bone chicken drumsticks. Breast meat might be the easy option, but the taste and texture of leg or thigh is a world apart... Yes, I COOK. And my big thing is to produce a (non) takeaway that is better and tastier than I ever get presented with when we order in.

Thai curries are a specific favorite - John is an Irish man and he loves his spuds, so the idea of a Thai curry with potato as an official ingredient is a must; he loves it, as do I! The spice mix/paste is always completely home-made - the secret is to mince your onion, garlic, lemongrass, ginger, chili and turmeric in a big batch, bag it up in sandwich bags and freeze until the desire for a yellow curry arises! Come on guys this takes twenty minutes to produce in the food processor, and you can forget the idea that shop purchased jars of cook-in sauces are actually acceptable - they are NOT! Whatever day of the week, there should be pride in what we cook, especially in what we cook for others. The curry sauce is at the heart of the meal and, of course, the marinade. I always make the gravy (curry sauce) in bulk and freeze in useable portions. The same is to be said for both 'Channa' (chickpea curry) and Dal (Yellow lentil curry).

I make a very mean chapati (flat bread), very thin and light, but to be truthful, paratha is our preference and honestly, you shouldn't bother to make it from scratch because to buy it in frozen, pre-rolled dough makes so much sense! It's really easy to defrost a Channa, and half of the defrosted curry sauce makes a Mutter (pea curry), and the other half is delicious with large red prawns. This is more like the real taste of India, very different to the usual Indian eateries here in the UK that fill their standard menu of sauces with vegetable oil to 'bulk them out'. I actually stopped ordering-in Indian food a few years ago as I was sick of being up half the night with indigestion. It is the reaction of the oil with the spice that creates indigestion, not the spice alone, so just omit the vegetable oil. Knowing too, that the entire meal was made with just two teaspoons of oil - duh! You can rest assured that it is healthy, and so much tastier too!

A roast dinner is usually the Sunday finale of the week, including home-made gravy with steamed/sautéed Savoy cabbage and on occasion, deep fried 'torn potatoes' opposed to the usual roasties. Here's how I do it:

Shred a Savoy cabbage, with the omission of the hard, veiny bit, and place in a frying pan with a good spoonful of butter and a little water, salt and pepper. Cover with the lid and steam first for maybe ten minutes, stirring occasionally. When the water has evaporated and the leaf is tender - but still with a slight bite - you're there! Just sauté for a few additional minutes and serve.

Now, 'Torn Potatoes?' you might ask! Just microwave Maris Pipers or King Edwards (in their skins) for however long they take to cook and leave to cool a little. Remove the skins and cup both of your hands around the skinless potato, then apply slight pressure towards the sides and slowly push until the potato breaks into two halves (practice makes perfect). Then break each half into two or three wedges lengthwise. And there you have it - torn potatoes. You can shallow fry and turn after the underside is Golden brown - but if you dare to deep fry, go for it!

After a lifetime of caution on deep fat frying - I remember my father's dependency on it - we only deep fry or sauté maybe twice a week at the very most, ((John and I). I recently purchased my first ever deep fat fryer, and the multiple ridges of the torn cooked potatoes give a much larger surface area, so cooked at a high temperature these are the best potatoes you are ever likely to eat!

Chapter Six
March

"She didn't quite know what the relationship was between lunatics and the moon, but it must be a strong one, if they used a word like that to describe the insane."
— Paulo Coelho, <u>Veronika Decides to Die</u>

My Sony Vaio computer packed up a couple of years ago, and we got an external hard drive casing which turned out to be rubbish! It simply didn't work. Another 'Made in China' disappointment, so apologies for great Japanese design (Toshiba hard drive) and a reality check that it is always down to the weakest link - the badly made Chinese casing.

What has been on that computer hard drive for the last six years? Photos of course, pictures of the girls as babies, and videos aplenty. Now our other guys (as small new-borns) are all stored and protected on my iPhone, thanks to the cloud concept; a new iPhone downloads your previous phone's data so you should never lose it. But the girls' baby photos were backed up on my old Sony laptop - and one day the girls and I sat down to retrieve all of the pictures.

Too many memories flooded back to me, yet it was all new and exciting for our two beautiful daughters, who were about to celebrate their sixth birthday. Time has flown by, and yet I always seem to coexist with the memories of all that happened.

I was honest, reactionary and truthful. We sat there for an hour or so and were aghast with each and every file full of baby photos that we opened; with each one we looked at I was reliving that time again, remembering our surrogate Rehanna and how she had helped John and me to have children; how small our babies were, with the tiniest of hands that curled around my fingers, and each with strands of dark brown hair. Flashbacks of individual memories of that time and place sped through my mind, and with each one I was reliving the sights and smells and noises.

It wasn't always like that - when I returned from India five years ago, all I wanted was to forget those agonising reminders of the anguish I had to go through to get our girls home. But we did get home after eight long and frustrating months, full of red tape and ridiculous obstructions at every turn. And now here we are, a very happy family filled with affection for one another.

The girls were aware that it is only women that have the ability to grow babies in their tummies and that their two dads are most certainly not women. The conversation was light and enough was included to make no secret of the special way that the girls came to us. Rehanna was our surrogate in India and is certainly part of our story

A couple of weeks after that, sitting at the dinner table, the subject was mentioned again. John and I had promised ourselves that when the children were old enough to ask questions, we would be as honest as possible. So, we continued the conversation about babies and the tummies that they grow within. The girls were very inquisitive about their origins and brought up the name Rehanna; I was completely open and used the word 'Surrogate' to describe her participation. The girls are very aware that Daddy and Dadda planned to have children, and that babies grow inside a woman's tummy, and that it takes three elements to make a baby! Even if you are a regular couple you need an egg, some fertiliser and a tummy. In the case of a boy girl couple, clearly the girl adds twice, but in our case, a third party provided the tummy.

To be honest, I didn't imagine having 'The Conversation' quite yet, but questions need answers and, on that day, we answered just a couple of those questions. I certainly don't want any animosity or feelings that we had held back the truth to our children in later life. Thor and the younger twins' surrogates were also mentioned by name, Ausa and Susheila. I thank all three of them from the bottom of my heart.

The clinic that created our embryos, using our 'DNA' and the anonymous egg donation, paid the surrogate about 35% of the overall fees, a significant and life changing amount, and equivalent to several years' wages in India. I would also like to add that all three women already had children of their own. Our full uncensored story, 'Eighteen Moons' is available to purchase through your Amazon account.

We had a particular day recently when the naughtiness could only be described as completely 'loco' (Spanish for crazy). The main commotion began in the garden in the morning. Daddy got them all into their shoes - I think every single dratted pair of shoes, wellies, sandals, and boots that had been in the shoe cupboard were strewn throughout the ground floor and then some. I seldom complain about picking up, it's all part of the job, but I pick up constantly and I do tire of the sheer volume that seems to be normal at the weekends.

Anyhow, by the time I had finished picking up and got all of the shoes back in the cupboard, I looked up and saw Tara and Thor running around the garden like wild things, half naked, and covered in water and mud and soapy bubbles. Caleb was sitting in a mud bath at the edge of the lawn, and Amritsar had a bucket of water and was about to pour it over Aaliyah's head... John had left the children to their own devices in the garden and - surprise surprise! - the water they were collecting from the downstairs WC was for mud pies. Not any old mud pies, but bubble mud pies! John said that the children said that I had said that it was all right to use the soap dispenser - and he believed them!!!

We rounded them up and started taking them upstairs ready for a shower. At that point, Sindy our nanny rang the doorbell. She had very kindly sewn on 'Chicky's' hat (Caleb's soft toy) and was delivering him back to us. When she came in and saw the five of them standing on the stairs, filthy from head to toe, she was horrified at the extent of the turmoil. She went upstairs and gave John a hand for the next fifteen minutes. It was at about that time that Remus began projectile vomiting his dinner around the living room floor. My head just sank into my lap!

The next day, whilst I was in the kitchen preparing some lunch, Caleb killed the Robot, Johns vacuum-cleaning birthday present. He came in from the living room, clenching the robot vacuum-cleaner tightly, and then he decided to throw it onto the kitchen floor! Pieces of it scattered and he just looked at me with an almighty grin on his face.

'Why did you do that' I asked.

'Sorry,' was his reply, and at least he had the decency to look a bit shamefaced. His two favourite words are 'Sorry' and 'Okay'. Thankfully the Robot was pieced back together, but believe me when I say, everything gets broken sooner or later in our house, and with the not so famous five, sooner is a more probable outcome.

After cleaning the lunch things away, I went into the living room; I was a bit suspicious because the not so famous five had been fairly quiet. As soon as I opened the door, Aaliyah ran away from where she had been standing in front of the television set, and Thor immediately ratted on her. 'It was Aaliyah! Aaliyah! She did it!' I wasn't sure what he was talking about for a second, but then the sun broke through, shone through the window and reflected off the television screen. Drat! The entire top third of the screen was scratched deeply, obviously with the blunt pencil that Aaliyah was still holding in her hand! I turned the television on to make sure it still worked, and it did, but it was almost unwatchable and the deeply set scratches were really off-putting. Tara instantly decided we needed a new TV. I immediately gave Aaliyah a good talking to and she was banished to 'The Thinking Chair' for ten minutes. She had recently done the same to the Aga fridge, and the Aga label on the cooker itself was broken and snapped in half by her mischievous hands! She knows when she is being naughty and always says that she wants to be good, but there is never any true remorse, and the cycle just repeats itself.

You knew that sooner or later the word 'vomit' would rear its ugly head, didn't you? Thor had been to a birthday party where he ate and ate and ate; then he came home and devoured the sweeties from his party bag, and then he eagerly devoured a cheese and ham roll. There were chocolate cupcakes, but as they were all full, especially Thor, they all had a taster bit of one cupcake divided into five. After their baths, Thor sat on the chaise and looked blankly into space, his tooth brush was in his mouth, motionless. Within the blink of an eye, it had fallen to the floor and gush after gush of sick oozed onto the dark oak flooring, splattering as it did so and creeping down between the floorboards...

Post 'projectile vomiting' on Sunday, the week began with calm before it dawned on us: Thor's being sick was not just down to his extreme gorging, but rather a stomach bug that had been introduced into the delicate eco system that is our family home. Monday passed by with no symptoms, however Tuesday morning was quite a different affair indeed! Thor woke me at 5 a.m. saying that his bed was wet. I checked and all seemed fine. But I turned to look into the entrance to the girls' room and noticed Tara out of bed and on the floor. Thor returned to his slumber and I headed in to see what was concerning Tara. 'Kit Koala is wet' she informed me and then she ushered my hand to feel the bedsheet. It was slightly damp, so I offed the sheet in an instant to reveal a myriad of books and knickknacks beneath her duvet. The duvet was dry as was her pillow so I set her up a bed on the fluffy carpet and inquired as to her stash of bed clutter. She had nothing to say in her defense. There were a few mutterings but basically all were comfortable, though I didn't check Caleb as all was silent in the semi darkness of the boys' room.

After Sindy arrived in the morning she went upstairs to help get the children up, and returned to the kitchen twenty-five minutes later clutching Tara's bedsheet plus all of Caleb's bedding. 'You should have seen it' she remarked, 'it was like the third world war!' Then she added, 'Caleb's bed was completely pebble-dashed!'

Day One of Lockdown had begun...

At the breakfast table everyone enjoyed their cornflakes though Tara and Caleb were slower eaters than normal. Tara was the first to look to the floor and empty her stomach. In very quick succession Caleb followed suit. Both Sindy and I jumped to action and calmed the two before cleaning up and disinfecting the said areas. The others, spoons halfway to their mouths, looked on in astonishment. 'That's a day home from school,' I told them. 'Me too, me too, Dadda' Thor piped up! 'I don't think so,' I added. The healthy three all went off to school with Sindy, and we at home settled in with Netflix. Within half an hour Caleb had vomited on himself twice, and on the large cushion they sit on beside the television, thrice. Happy Days. A mammoth washing followed, as you can imagine, what with the soiled towels, bed linen, and masses of children's clothing.

Day two of Lockdown...

All was well with the two in quarantine, which meant they were all back at school on Day three, and normality returned to The Shires.

Winter had finally come to an end and I could see in the garden that life was reasserting itself; spring saw me spending more time out there, and I gazed in wonder at some of the budding shrubs just beginning to loosen their tight grip on new life and growth from within, pushing so hard to spring forth. The terrace had seen several hours of attention during the course of a few days, and getting it ready for the summer was considerably hard work, but it was beginning to look like a place where we could enjoy what the summer would have to offer. Lots of warm sunshine I was hoping. It's a great place for barbequing and chilling so fingers crossed on the weather front. I'm looking forward to seeing those spring buds blossoming and blooming into beautiful and colourful flowers.

We were gearing up for the girls' birthday in a few days' time. Tesco delivered a shed-load of stuff including forty 200g chocolate bars that I had ordered; I'd planned to remove the wrappers and re-brand them for the party bags. They also delivered, amongst other things, £10 worth of ingredients for the adult catering for the party. 'Indian Veg Cuisine' was the theme for the grownups nosh and I was planning to cater for forty adults for just a tenner! Yes, really!

The girls awoke on their birthday one year older, and they were very happy indeed to be six years old. We were having a celebration on the day, but 'The Big Party' was to be held the following Saturday in conjunction with a school friend, Pip. While Sindy went to collect them from school and take them to the park for an hour, I dressed the kitchen table for the '6 Today Extravaganza'. Their main gifts from John and me were new tablets, since all four devices we have (the children's that is), were by then broken and wouldn't charge. We realised that this might be partially down to them having been given headphones, the jack of which they had tried to plug into the wrong hole. A circular peg does not fit into that of a rectangle!

I was really looking forward to seeing the girls' faces when they unceremoniously tore the paper from the pile of gifts, wrapped in colour-coded paper, but at the last minute I realised I hadn't decorated the birthday cake! That was a panic, but I had it done just before they all piled back into the house. John was late home from work so he missed the frenzied present-opening and the candle blowing, but the children stayed up late to see him and didn't get to bed til nearly ten o'clock!

The next day I was busy cutting open the Tesco 200g bars of dark, milk and white chocolate for rewrapping in foil and applying our personalised 'Thank You' labels, ready to be put in party bags at the weekend for the 'Big Party' revelers. The theme was 'Wild Animal Party', and I wasn't sure what the entertainer was going to bring, probably a parrot and a rabbit! But I hoped it would be enough to entertain forty children for at least two hours! It got me to thinking though... in my day, if we were lucky enough to have a birthday party, we invited a few friends on the day itself, or maybe the closest weekend; we were given a few crappy gifts, danced to pop music, played 'Pass the Parcel' and that was that! We were happy with it and didn't expect anything more.

Anyhow, I carried on with the preparations, and the second big 'Bake Off' cake was created in the afternoon; it was a triple tier chocolate cake, internally moistened with Dadda's home-made strawlime berry jam, and frosted externally with home-made ganache. I even made home-made white chocolate pyramids to adorn the top! Bloody hell, how times have changed! Renting a hunting lodge, hiring an entertainer, catering for forty adults to luncheon for under a tenner (that was my cost saving initiative, it can be done!) and picnic lunch boxes for the mass of children. It seems that all of us parents have to participate in this frivolity when it comes to the 'Special Day' that is a birthday party for our child or, in the case of twins, children.

Saturday, the 'Big Party' day began early. There was excitement in the air, starting with a bed invasion at 6 a.m., and soon afterwards a breakfast of pancakes with Dadda's home-made mango jam drizzled liberally with a splash of lime juice. Sindy and sister Sally came in to make up the lunchboxes at 9 a.m., jam, and ham, sandwiches, the jam on this occasion was black grapple. Pips mum Thea arrived at 11 a.m. when they all went off together to dress the venue with a multitude of animal related decor and an explosion of balloons.

I cooked a mass of perfectly cooked basmati rice in the microwave. Our three veg curries were precooked and bagged up in the refrigerator (Mutter, Dal and Channa) and thirty chapattis were dry cooked on the griddle. Wrapped in a wet tea towel and polythene bag to keep moist, they were added to the bags of food that were set to leave with Sindy and Sally for the setup at the hunting lodge where the party was being held. I was very pleased that I had managed to make the curries for a tenner - it's just as well I no longer put an hourly, monetary rate on my time invested in the things I do. I would surely be disenchanted, wouldn't I? Welcome to parenthood.

We all arrived later to meet Thea and her hubby John (Pips parents) who were also helping to set up. During the next fifteen minutes forty excited children and their parents arrived and the noise increased to a deafening level, with squeals and shrieks and children running around. Before we knew it, the party was in full swing. The wild animal lady and her assistant managed to hold their attention while they entertained the little ones with face painting and balloon animals, and afterwards everyone had a great time eyeing the myriad of surprisingly scary creatures; shrieking and screeching ensued, and hiding behind 'skirts', with each creature that the animal lady produced, including Madagascan hissing cockroaches, stick insects, geckos, and even a tarantula or two!

The children consumed their lunch boxes and the grownups devoured the 'Pur Veg' curries with gusto. Sindy and Sally were fantastic, as were our fellow hosts, keeping all the children under control and making sure everyone was happy and had enough to eat. The hunting lodge was a brilliant venue and we left with a happy crowd having appreciated that it was a more inclusive affair - the grownups and their enjoyment are often an oversight at these events. Catering for forty adults for a tenner went down well, I think. And a few of them even thanked us for a party that was a party for all and not just the children. Job well done! The other matter was my shock at the gratuitous amount of presents and cards this year. I just counted a mass of cards between the twins and as for the avalanche of presents on the dining hall table - unbelievable!

Oh -and the forty hand-wrapped, personally printed 'thank you' chocolate bars looked really good.

Okay, on the subject of Birthday Cakes, I'm your man! There are seven to bake every year in our house and we all love them! Sadly, we have only one small fan-assisted oven that works on our Aga, so I have to cook each twelve-inch diameter layer one at a time.

I use grams for all measurements in weight except for making cakes. The old imperial weight of ounces is my choice when I'm baking. Forget your kilos and grams and a cup of this and a cup of that – it's all totally alien to me. For a cake it's simple, 6+6+6+3 (6 oz sugar, 6oz softened butter, 6 oz self-raising flour, and 3 eggs) is the winning formula!

In your food processor firstly blitz 6oz sugar and 6oz softened butter. When this looks smooth, drop in one egg at a time whilst still mixing. Turn off a minute after the third egg has dropped, then add the flour, a splash of vanilla essence, and a good pinch of salt.

Blitz again until smooth and velvety. If making chocolate cake, substitute one and a half of the ounces of flour with cocoa powder, and hold on the vanilla essence.

I do this three times in all, each time baking in the centre of my oven at 170 degrees centigrade for twenty minutes. I always use Dadda's Jam to sandwich the layers together. For vanilla cake I use raspberry or strawberry, and usually blackcurrant or cherry jam for the chocolate cake.

Sometimes I frost with home-made buttercream, but I prefer to lavish the cake with home-made chocolate ganache. Just boil double cream and throw in as much dark chocolate as you dare (you can Google for exact ratios). Allow to firm up in the fridge overnight then bring the ganache back to room temperature in order to embellish that sticky, jammy sponge. Well, that's all I've got to say about Birthday Cakes!

And I must add, nobody – and I mean NOBODY – has ever complained about one of my home-made Birthday Cakes!

Chapter Seven
April

"I'm over the MOON when I'm under WATER."
—Unknown

There is real love between Aaliyah and our adorable Dalmatian hound Gracie. She really does get overlooked a lot of the time, Gracie that is, not Aaliyah, because with Remus's rather robust behaviour, he is certainly the 'Top Dog' in our house; saying that, Gracie does try to assert herself now and again, and very occasionally, she succeeds!

About a year ago Aaliyah's traumatic-threes kind of slowed down a notch! It's true that I was sending her to the naughty chair rather a lot, but then, as if by magic, her continual antagonism just slowed down and she became a rather more mellowed little girl. At the same time, she started to show our two Dalmatians, Remus and Gracie, an awful lot of attention, especially Gracie (a girl thing I guess). Ever since, every day, the two can be seen playing from time to time. It's fascinating to watch as Aaliyah holds Gracie by the neck with her little arms outstretched to minimise the licks, and they just play together, with Gracie trying, usually unsuccessfully, to lick Aaliyah's face, and Aaliyah ducking and giggling. Maybe this love could be nurtured into something very positive! Of course, her behavior, Aaliyah's not Gracie's, still found her sat on the naughty chair, but not nearly as much as it used to!

Aaliyah really wanted to be good but, as you may have realised, remorse was in rather short supply when it came to her antics. She bit Caleb one day, and I thought it was an isolated incident; she knew it was wrong, she knows it's not acceptable, she was told she mustn't do it. The very next day she bit him again! She showed no consideration for the consequences whatsoever. It really sucks to be regarded as lower in the general pecking order and poor Caleb cried; thankfully Sindy gave the 'Bad Cop' response and sat Aaliyah on the 'Thinking Chair'. Then, given her angry and uncontrollable vexing, she was sent up to bed early, and she stomped noisily up the stairs in protest. I was upset that, with all of the improvements in her behaviour in the recent months, we felt that we were back to square one. It was so disheartening. Sindy and I reassured each other that she was still only three years old, almost four, but remorse was still very sadly lacking. She's a pretty little thing, and looks like butter wouldn't melt in her mouth!

One of the local villages held their annual Easter Fayre, and 'Dadda's Jams' took a stall. This left poor Daddy to traipse around the muddy field with the children on the Easter Egg Hunt, searching high and low for the Easter Egg tokens. Caleb was surprisingly clingy with me, a thing that he in general, is not. But then I got the full picture when I realised, after seeing him gaze longingly at them, that part of the stall set-up had three bonbon dishes overflowing with home-made candies. Humph, I felt that he was there more for the gluttony of sugary treats than to purely hang out with his Dadda! I want to say thank you to the great people there for a brilliant day out for all of the children, and especially to those who indulged in the purchase of some of 'Dadda's Jams'. A few people quizzed me as to why I was making home-made Jams, and it was interesting to remember that it was largely thanks to the children attending preschool that, each weekday morning, I had three hours of free time to fill. And Dadda likes to get Jammin'!

It was the second day of the Easter Break when Thor's itchy head lead to an investigation by Sindy; she uncovered what is commonly known as nits, or head lice, within our family. A second dratted infestation for us. As before, it was an immediate strip off and into the shower.

'But why Dadda, why?'

'Because, Thor, your head is crawling with lice and we need to get rid of them!'

'Noooo, they're mine!' Thor jumped about, hands in his hair as if trying to stop his head from falling off! He loves to covet things, and most of the time we indulge, but I'll be blowed if he's going to hang on to those nasty little creepy-crawlies.

'Now, Thor! And the rest of you, come on...'

The not so famous five were not impressed at having an impromptu shower and head scrub, but the situation was remedied within an hour as there were two bottles of 'Hedrin' in the cupboard, left over from the last invasion. So as soon as they appeared, the little buggers had completely vanished (I hoped). Thank you Sindy for your speedy intervention. If this had come at a weekend, I am sure that the drama and chaos would have been much, much greater. As for Thor, I think he was the perpetrator...

Well, Tara was beside herself with the falling out of her second tooth later that night, and I'm glad I was there for the event, since I had missed the first one. Obviously, it was too late for the tooth fairy to come then, so the next night was the big night for our ever-elusive, mystical visitor. That would actually be John, as I would be far too nervous of waking the sleeping crew, knowing I would tiptoe far too noisily through their rooms. I'm pleased to report that the big tooth growing behind looked sturdy enough.

Goodbye little tooth, goodbye!

As you know, Remus and Gracie are not averse to chasing the odd squirrel or three in the garden, but they are not the only wildlife to be seen out there! I won't mention birds as they are too many and plentiful throughout the year, though I will mention the occasional pairs of geese that fly over at this time of year. I've only seen mated pairs so far, and no squadrons like you see in the autumn when they choose to fly south, in perfect formation, for sunnier climes. Rabbits reappeared this year. Some years they are abundant, others nonexistent. It must be due to the awesome Red Kites that hunt in the area, or disease maybe. Mind you those Kites scarpered away with the neighbours tortoise last year! It was there one minute, munching on a lettuce leaf, and the next it was swept up by a mighty pair of talons, and was last seen being air lifted above the very green and leafy tree canopy and out of sight. Deer are another mammal that occasionally wander through the gardens and woodland, all year round; they are mesmerising to watch, though they are very coy and rather wary. I saw a family of five deer munching away at a neighbours' hedge last year, and they had managed to do a fair deal of damage before I disturbed them and they all bounded off into the woods.

It is usually at this time of year that I see the first of the local snake population come out of hibernation. There is a nest of these slithery reptiles within the limestone drywall on our terrace, not five metres from the back door, and there are not just one or two, but maybe twenty grass snakes of various ages and sizes, all hibernating throughout the winter months. The dogs go crazy sniffing around the two large cracks in the wall where they come and go, but they usually vanish for the summer to hunt in the grounds and woods nearby. One neighbour actually cultivated a wild flower meadow in order to study these rather secretive reptiles. A snake that resembled an adder (though I am not completely sure) did hiss at me whilst I was enjoying a cup of coffee last year. There are also a couple of species of rodents that nest nearby. Perfect food for our local predators, I guess. I've seen plenty of frogs around, a couple of newts, even a toad in the garden. There is a stream that meanders its way through the woods, so that explains that I suppose.

The odd, friendly pheasant can be seen in relatively close proximity, pottering in the grass and pecking for insects and leaves. On the insect side of things - they are finally back! Food for the birds and good pollinators. Six weeks ago, the midges appeared, five weeks ago, the bumblebees, four weeks back the first of the fly species, and I saw the first butterfly two weeks ago. Ladybirds aplenty all year really as they nest within the metal window frames of the upstairs bay window; they are a real pest in the springtime and autumn when they seem to amass in their hundreds! There are also the most magnificent dragonflies that seem to come and go in groups every summer, in various iridescent colours; I haven't spied them yet, it must still be a bit early, I think. And finally, I must add that I have not seen a fox as yet in The Shires. This sly but stunning predator is prolific in London where we used to live, beside the railway line; they seem to have lost their fear of humans and can readily be seen in urban gardens or wandering along the roads in the early hours, as bold as brass! Well, there you go!

The wonders of living the country life, here in The Shires of leafy England.

The holidays were zooming by. That, plus I am not looking forward to four days of Sundays, with the only pacifier for the children being chocolate eggs. They've already scoffed their milk chocolate bunnies; that leaves just five more chocolate eggs each to munch through. I purchased two each thinking that would be plenty, but then one for each child came back with John from Dublin, Sindy gave them one apiece, and finally Sally and Sonia (Sindy's sister and mum) have brought one for each of them too.

It was a couple of days before Easter, the little ones were in bed, and I had just settled down with a deep sigh, looking forward to a quiet few hours, when frantic shouting upstairs had me rushing to the top floor. Caleb had been playing on Tara's bed, thankfully the bottom of the two bunk beds, and he had just fallen off of it. His coordination isn't the best as you might recall, but somehow, he fell out of the bed and got his arm trapped between the slats on the side of the bed. He was very distressed; his face was tearstained and he was giving big gulping sobs; I could tell he was shocked. I asked the other children to stay in the bedroom whilst I took him downstairs; they were very somber, and I think they realised the seriousness of the situation. I wanted to carry Caleb, but felt I might hurt him if I tried to pick him up, so I led him carefully down the stairs, talking gently and trying to calm him down. He had removed his pyjama top and it was clear that his arm had been broken. His arm, about one third up from his wrist, looked odd, and was bent at about a fifteen-degree angle. I'm no doctor, but I thought it might have been a clean break.

John wasn't home as he was in London for a leaving-do at work, so, in complete desperation, I called Sindy. She arrived within twenty minutes and took Caleb to the Accident and Emergency department at our local hospital. I stayed home and waited for her update, wishing all the time that I could have gone too. I settled the four remaining children into bed whilst trying to have that chat about 'Cause and Effect'; they seemed to understand that, whatever they do, there will always be consequences. But they are all still so little, remember, and I'm not sure that the little ones do learn from their mistakes as they tend to repeat their bad behaviour. I was very saddened by the traumatic day.

Sindy arrived back home with Caleb at 12.30 a.m.; he was very tired and pale, and wanted to go straight up to bed. Sindy reassured me that all was well, and she had thoughtfully photographed the x-Ray so we could see it; he had to return to the hospital the following Thursday for another x-ray.

The following day, the little ones were meant to be having their afternoon nap, or at the very least some quiet time, after lunch (long gone were those magical moments of story time before sleepy bye byes etc.) but there was a good thirty minutes of commotion with little shrieks and the pitter-patter of running feet. I gave them the benefit of the doubt - and that was my first big mistake! Tara went to see what they were up to and came racing back down saying, 'Dadda, they have been very naughty - they have made a mess,' They've done this several times in the past, so I imagined that I would just venture up to the top floor and pick up all of the toys and clothing that would have been lying around. My second mistake was to wait for a few minutes before I reacted; it suddenly dawned on me that I could hear a cascade of water coming from John's and my bedroom, and I jumped to attention and flew up the stairs.

Charging into our bedroom I saw a steady flow of water coming through the light fixture; it was making a pool below, and I quickly turned and sped up the second flight of stairs. Aaliyah heard me and made a swift retreat to her bed, leaving the boys, an overflowing sink, a running tap, several sopping wet towels and wet clothing scattered to the four corners of their shower room and surrounding area. They were naked, laughing, and running amok without a care. I shouted lots, so much in fact my throat was later rather sore. All I could do, after turning off the tap and taking the plug out of the sink, was to remove the soaking wet items and mop up the pool beside my bed on the floor below.

The next day water was still dripping onto the living room floor from a big wet patch on the ceiling. Not the best of days! But thankfully Caleb was well (arm in plaster cast), though I've threatened no Chocolate Egg for the little ones unless behaviour improves! Amritsar and Tara were gloating.

Easter Sunday saw our planned afternoon Easter Egg hunt cancelled! In the morning we tidied and manicured the terrace in preparation for the hunting and finding of hidden chocolate (which wasn't yet hidden!). All was quiet; I sunbathed on the lawn for half an hour while John looked after and played with the not so famous five. They were playing happily on the terrace when John had to go inside to take a couple of phone calls. He was gone for 'just a few minutes', he said, but came back out to complete disaster! There was a quagmire of water, sand, and mud everywhere. Plant pots had been emptied of their contents. Mud was covering all of the children from head to toe! Even the dogs had mud patches and muddy paws!

As soon as I heard John let out a shout, I came running, but stopped short when I saw the scene. I'm afraid Daddy and Dadda raised their voices! After the events of the other day, with the three little ones destroying the ceilings on two separate floors with water, yes - water had again played its part in the cancelling of 'A Fun Day'. And it seemed that Tara, looking the guiltiest, had been the ringleader!

Caleb and Daddy had to go back to the hospital, 25 miles away, and expected a long wait in Accident and Emergency. The reason being a sopping wet plaster cast! In the end they weren't too long getting the plaster reset, partly because Caleb is such a cutie that the nurse fell for his smile. No sooner had they checked in and were told a 3 - 4 hour wait, than the nurse said, 'I can probably smuggle him through if you follow me now!' I believe the woman who did the casting wasn't busy, just one other there at the time and she was almost done with him.

The afternoon came, and everywhere looked as if world war three had left us a scarred battlefield. By 3.30 p.m. the children were all sat in their jimjams watching television, and they were relatively quiet. An ever-bigger pile of laundry sat in the kitchen. Sunday, slow roast shoulder of lamb and roast potatoes were much delayed. But oh! The bliss of them being quiet! The children enjoyed a ham sandwich and a Hobnob (from a packet) for dinner, then all five of them had an early night. Five children, all under the age of six, has its drawbacks. An older chap or chapette might just lead them with a little more caution than 'Tara's enthusiasm' did on that Easter Sunday morning.

The story did not quite finish when they went up to bed after their sandwiches. They continued their loud, rapscallion antics for a further hour, and I ended up, having had enough, storming up to the top floor. I came to a halt in the doorway; I was thoroughly dismayed and shocked when I saw the sheer devastation of their rooms! If our nanny Sindy is reading this - I'm so sorry, but I guess they know not what they do. They seemingly had no remorse. Amritsar and Aaliyah were quiet and in bed so they were told that there would indeed be an egg for them tomorrow, but sadly, Tara, leading the destruction, was told 'No Egg,' as were the boys. She looked sick with guilt, or maybe she was just distraught with the realisation of not getting a chocolate egg the next day. Thor just screamed for twenty minutes 'Sorry Dadda, Sorry'. I left them to it and said they were not allowed to come down for breakfast the next morning until they tried their hardest to tidy up their rooms.

Later, when all was really quiet, John and I enjoyed slow roast shoulder of lamb, roast potatoes alongside, cooked in the meat juices, spinach (my new favourite vegetable), with very thin green beans and, wait for it - John's home-grown asparagus! Yes – home grown! It was delicious! The really sad thing was that the children would never actually know or care about what they had missed out on.

Their behaviour seemed to be getting worse. It really does sadden me when they just don't learn that there are always repercussions. And on that day, in between two altercations, I had the most memorable moment with Thor. He said to me, "Dadda, can I whisper something to you'? 'Yes,' I replied, and he went on to whisper, 'Dadda, I really, really love you.' It brought a tear to my eye.

It's funny how food transports us back to a moment or a place. Just by making the choice of samosas, rather than my usual sandwich and crisps, I find myself taken back to the hustle and bustle, the thronging streets of Mumbai. Towards the end of my time on the Indian Sub-Continent, I often shared my time with a taxi driver known as Ram. He was a 'kind hearted' fellow, something that was very sadly in short supply in those times. On our many trips to the Foreigners Regional

Registration Office (FRRO), he would show me both sympathy and support. He would also sing ancient songs in Hindi that, with his whispering, reedy voice, had the effect of halting my tears and making me stop worrying about what was happening in the 'NOW' and transport me to a mindset of relative serenity. Maybe more about remembering the trips to the FRRO on another occasion, but for now it's all about samosas. Ram and I would always stop at one or two street vendors and enjoy a lunch, or afternoon tiffin of samosas, with a small cup of extremely sweet, milky tea. He had a very good heart. And I will never be able to eat a samosa ever again without him in my thoughts.

Samosas are one of my absolute favourite Indian snacks. Any tiffin box would quite simply be incomplete without one (or two) of these spiced moreish delights! I personally like mine filled with chicken tikka or potato masala, chopped up finely. It's all about choices isn't it? Having said that, the traditional veg filling is so easy to throw together, so that's what I'm cooking up. Right, one other consideration, and that is: filo pastry or white sliced bread? Of course, there's a water/flour dough recipe that's also traditional, very easy, but you can Google that one as I am going with white sliced bread.

Firstly, make your veg mixture. One onion, a drizzle of oil and two teaspoons of Garam masala, fry on a light heat for a few minutes, and maybe throw in some mustard seed. These are optional, but if you do, beware the eruption of popping seeds after a minute in the pan! Add frozen peas and cook for a few more minutes; lastly, add finely chopped cooked potatoes and season to taste. That's it, allow to cool. Now here comes the fun bit! With a rolling pin, roll out and flatten your slices of bread. Apply some weight - you want the bread as flat as cardboard. Trim off the crusts and cut diagonally. Mix a little water with some flour in a cup or a small bowl to make your glue! Take your triangle and make a cone shape and use your glue to seal the edge. Fill with a couple of teaspoons of mixture being careful not to overfill. Finally use your 'glue' to seal down the flap tightly. Repeat this as many times as your mixture allows. Now deep fry until golden brown. Forget about the calories, this is fried food at its best. If it makes you feel any better, pat dry with plenty of kitchen towel and enjoy! Bliss!

Chapter Eight
May

"In my defence, the moon was full and I was left unsupervised."
- Unknown

After a run of particularly bad behaviour, Aaliyah was told that if she could be good for a week, she could have her very own iPad (Amazon Fire 7). She was indeed a very, very good girl; there had been a couple of grumples along the way, but she realised what she was doing, pulled herself up by the bootstraps, and tried to behave again - we were very impressed. Tara had been binge-watching some ninety episodes of 'Dragons' rather than playing games on her tablet, and she very kindly allowed Aaliyah to play with it. Aaliyah worked out a lot of the games all by herself, and seemed to be truly enjoying the learning aspect. She has definitely grown up a lot in these last six months. The eight days of being good must not stop there as she will have to continue this streak of good behaviour in order to actually spend time on her brand-new iPad! I think we've got this sussed... hehe.

On the morning of the eighth day she rushed down to the kitchen to see if there was anything for her. She had kept her part of the bargain, and now she was hoping we had kept our part too. There on the table, at her usual place, was a gift-wrapped package. She looked at me and Daddy, eyes wide, and we nodded. 'Go ahead, it's yours.' She climbed up onto the chair, ripped the paper off, and there it was! Her very own flashy, new Amazon Fire 7 tablet with a 'fuchsia' purple case, all set up with her very own profile and a pink unicorn as her motif. She was one very happy girl, and she had the biggest happiest grin imprinted from cheek to cheek as she hugged it to herself. Yes, we'd had a few fraught moments over that week, but she managed to keep a hold of herself and reign in her anger when, under normal circumstances, she would have screamed the house down.

Once Tara and Amritsar were back home from school the three girls huddled on one of the sofa's, and her two big sisters assisted Aaliyah in her selection of games and educational tools to download. It's win-win really as, in order to actually spend time on this new accessory, she will have to continue this streak of being good.

Shortly afterwards Thor was told that if he could also be good for one week, he would get a replacement iPad as well. But with Thor, seven hours would be an achievement, let alone seven days! I am looking forward to a near future when Thor is able to prove that he can be a good boy as well. Sadly, it will be some time before Caleb is a contender as his ability to break stuff (his left arm included) is just too great at this point in time. We can only wait and see what the future holds on that score!

After that we had a quiet few days. No really – we did! Summing it up, there had been no all-encompassing change of direction from our usual 'organised chaos,' but rather slightly less stress from the little ones. Thor was better behaved, though there was still the occasional steam whistling from his kettle, Caleb seemed to have calmed down a little, and Aaliyah was playing contentedly with her tablet.

Thor earned his iPad (Kindle 7) for three days of good behaviour, due to, let's say, a marked change in his outbursts. They still existed of course, but overall, he was a much better-behaved little boy. He was much more articulate and he certainly had shown within these last six months that, overall, he wanted to be good. Just like Aaliyah, there is a significant amount of hope that he ascends into the mantle of being a big boy (for Aaliyah, a big girl) and being able to start 'Big School' in September. We had, of course, considered Caleb's situation. It was difficult but, if you looked on the surface, he was trying so very hard. His diction was certainly getting better, though his ability to articulate at the dinner table, without slouching or dropping more than he consumed! Well, we were still in two minds...

Go straight to jail. Do not pass go, do not collect £200. But did they earn a 'Get Out of Jail Free' card?

We had a delicious home-made lunch of potato and watercress soup, and freshly baked baguette smothered with butter, so we were not exactly starving. The children had been very well behaved, displaying good manners and eating nicely, and I thought it would be safe for me to leave them while I popped upstairs to sort out a couple of things. John had already ventured out to the garden for fifteen minutes for some Spring sunshine; this left the fruit bowl unguarded!

A shout upstairs from Amritsar asking for an apple for each of them was followed by a 'Yes' reply from myself. Ten minutes later I returned to find Thor and Caleb munching down on two bananas, and the floor was scattered with banana skins. I could have acted out a comedy-sketch banana-skin joke at that point, but I didn't!

'You asked for apples!' I said.

'We only ate apples,' our three girls piped up.

'And what about the boys?' I asked.

Neither could reply for mouths completely bloated with banana. I looked at what had been a full fruit bowl, now slimmed down to just four 'ripening' pears – all of the apples and bananas were gone. 'Who ate the bananas?' I queried.

'Thor and Caleb,' Tara replied (she's very good like that).

I won't script the rest of the conversation, but the boys were told that for eating all five bananas between them (after their apples) and denying the girls of their bananas, the boys would have no dinner that night!

'But I'm hungry,' Thor piped up. 'I'm still hungry.'

I explained that there are always consequences in what we do and that just taking things was not allowed in our house. However, Thor was adorable for the rest of the afternoon, and Caleb was less naughty than his average weekend day, so I thought they had earned their 'Get Out of Jail Free' card. Subsequently, they later enjoyed a smoky bacon spag-bol with trottole vert and a snowstorm of Parmesan cheese.

On another matter, it's a real bugger not being able to drive. It seems that, in this respect, Sindy is very heavily relied upon. She did not take her morning off, but instead took Caleb back to the hospital for his plaster cast to be removed. Woohoo! He would be a regular little boy again, one without a broken arm. They didn't get back until after the school run and I had really been looking forward to seeing Calo without his arm in plaster, and hoping hard that in future he would try to be a little less ballistic. But trying to tell a three-year-old to 'take it easy' is in itself not an easy ask.

And then Thor lost MiMi, his very best bear. Drat! He was very upset, and we had absolutely no idea where MiMi could be; John and I had looked high and low, and in every nook and cranny we could think of, but to no avail. During the midst of the week-long hunt, Thor – 'The Coveter' - returned from preschool clutching about half a dustbin-worth of litter, all piled into a broken cardboard box. He wouldn't put it down for a while, just held on to it tightly and refused to let anyone touch it. He finally gave in in order to eat, and enjoyed his chicken sandwich with Dadda's home-made tomato chutney. When he finally finished, he grabbed his pile of jumble and headed for the stairs. I spotted him just in time and stopped him in his tracks. 'Thor! No! That junk is not going upstairs!' He reluctantly left it on the floor at the bottom of the stairs while he, Aaliyah and Caleb enjoyed their midday rest.

Afterwards, back downstairs and clutching the box of rubbish, with not too many mentions of 'where's MiMi' the little ones had a trip to the park with Sindy before picking up the girls from school. Thor was allowed to take his tray of recyclables to the park. I took Sindy aside before they left; 'Please, Sindy,' I implored. 'Please can we lose the pile of rubbish somewhere along the way?' She was very good and put it in the boot of the car while the children played in the playground, and left it there afterwards, to be discarded on tomorrow's school run - in a public bin. We couldn't risk putting it in the bin at home, you see, because Thor checks our recycle bag at home on a regular basis!

We really had looked everywhere for MiMi, even the watering can in the garden. We have discovered that Thor liked to put MiMi in secret places - a shoe box, a paper bag, in fact any place where he felt MiMi would be comfortable and safe - afterwards he always completely forgot where poor MiMi might be... Last time MiMi went missing, he was found two weeks later in a draw in our bedroom.

After seven days of searching with no luck, and with Thor getting increasingly distressed, MiMi was finally unearthed. He ran into the kitchen waving MiMi above his head, shouting 'Look Dadda, Look!' Thor was beside himself with joy and very proud to be the one that found him. Well, he was the one to have lost him after all! And guess where Thor's intrepid bear was hiding all of this time? He was discovered hiding in the piano stool, using sheet music for a blanket! Well, all is back as it should be. One very happy little boy and his most favourite bear ever.

For some time now the worry of Mrs Snodgrass's 'Naughty School' was not quite enough when it came to rectifying babyish behaviour. Something that all of our little ones did on a fairly regular basis. Neither Mrs Snodgrass nor Bettina (Mrs Snodgrass's assistant) were cut out to deal with small children who acted like babies. You know, when a three- or four-year-old is still constantly sucking on fingers or thumbs?

Caleb, bless him, was still finding his vocabulary, so in an attempt to get him to articulate a bit more – to go the extra distance, we instilled yet another threat. The worry of spending the summer at 'Baby Camp' had proved a winner. Baby camp was run by the fictional 'Mr Strickland'. His camp was one for little boys and girls who liked to act like babies (on a fairly regular basis). His dormitories were stacked high with cots that were five in number long and five in number high. These walls of cribs were essentially walls of bars and behind said bars were 'Baby Camp' inmates, young children who liked to act like babies! All that could be heard in Mr Strickland's dorms were baby cries and the sound of 'goo-goo gaa-gaa.' Now nobody wanted to spend the summer at 'Baby Camp', so just the mention of Mr Strickland's name was enough to stop any babylike behaviour in our house, at least for a while...

Aaliyah is a terror for sucking her fingers when she thinks nobody is looking! The other day, whilst Glenn Miller was playing Moonlight Serenade quietly in the background, everyone was settled playing with their tablets; it felt incredibly peaceful. Aaliyah had the big sofa to herself, with Gracie lying beside her, head on Aaliyah's knees. Without thinking, Aaliyah's fingers crept into her mouth. I called out to her and she instantly removed them. A moment later, they were back again, and again I called out to her and the hand was plonked down onto her lap. Seeing that I was watching, she made a big deal of teasing me, letting her fingers creep up her chin, almost into her mouth, and quickly away again, giggling, moving her fingers over her cheek towards her mouth, and quickly away again. 'Ah, ah, no!' I called to her, and she ignored me and carried on. Then I just said 'Mr Strickland!' and she collapsed into a fit of giggles and turned back to playing with her tablet. She's a rascal!

We knew that Aaliyah was definitely ready for 'Big School' – Mrs Snodgrass would be disappointed that her school for naughty children would miss out on Aaliyah's attendance, as would Mr Strickland from 'Baby Camp'. Please keep your fingers crossed in these coming summer months. I really want them to all start this new and exciting chapter together.

P.S. remember that Mrs Snodgrass and Mr Strickland are fictional characters!

Nearing the end of the month we decided that all of the children needed a haircut. Tara and Amritsar had their long brown hair trimmed neatly, and Thor's hair – not particularly long – was given a bit more of a style. Caleb and Aaliyah looked almost identical with masses of curly silver blonde hair; Aaliyah's was tidied and trimmed, and we decided Caleb needed a proper haircut. It was cut a lot shorter, and of all the children his was the most radical. He looks like a very grown up little boy now! I'm thinking a crew cut next time – maybe a flat top!

I've not talked about food of recent, so a few random thoughts...

What springs to mind is Greek Yogurt! 'Hold on the honey sweetie.' Dadda's home-made 'Strawlime Berry' Jam did the trick one night. A splash of water and a liberal drizzle, then a simple whirlpool made with a teaspoon and voila, a sweet treat for children and adults alike.

The children like 'Kiddies Cassoulet', a favorite of mine and theirs. It's really posh beans on toast. Easily made and scrummy too. Eight Irish sausages (cut up), one tin of Branston Baked Beans. Sorry for the defection Heinz, but yours taste too sweet (please drop the sugar content). A tin of chopped tomatoes, some seasoning and lots of freshly made breadcrumbs on top. Quick and easy.

Our favorite pizza is from Firezza, but I like to mimic - I make a great pizza dough, sauce and toppings. As for a Chinese menu, I will considerately reconstruct ingredients from our favorite dishes from Lee's Chinese takeaway in West London (special fried rice and prawn, chili and green beans are a particular favorite) - we don't really need to order in do we? Well, we're living in The Shires now! So, who cares?

Thai food is always a treat, but I guess that falls under the umbrella of curries, which I have talked about at length...

Fish and shellfish are always on the grownup's menu. My favourite is lobster Thermidor. No gruyere - just a cheese sauce with masses of grated extra mature cheddar. Coquille Saint Jacque Mornay (Scallops in Cheese Sauce) is another fave - fancy looking but fairly easy to make. And let's not forget those Argentinian Red Shrimp available at Iceland supermarkets! They're great just fried in butter and garlic with French Fries, or peeled, cooked, and used as a substitute for lobster meat. Prawns are also great served up with salmon.

I always have several portions of lobster bisque in the freezer - easily defrosted and used for a bouillabaisse or sauce with salmon and shrimp. Served with boiled or mashed potatoes, green beans or asparagus - yummy! There's another sauce I make for pasta as well as with fish and that's deglazing the pan you cooked the fish in with butter, double cream and a shed-load of Parmesan cheese, salt and pepper. For pasta I would add/fry finely chopped mushrooms and smoked salmon. Again, plenty of Parmesan cheese to garnish and some fresh parsley.

Bon Appetite!

Chapter Nine
June

"When the moon is at its best and the sun at its worst,
you have a hard time finding where's the nest and where's the bird!"
— Shweta Tale

The beginning of the month brought good news on the potty front. Caleb had been full on potty training for several days; of course, there had been a couple of mistakes, but we persevered. He needed to be dry before September and the onslaught of 'Big School' which was only two months away, so we were determined to get him ready in time. He asked to be back in a nappy after his mistakes, but we kept to the program. And I knew that he was committed to make this happen, just as we were!

Caleb's new hairdo certainly made him look more grown up - much less chaotic. And that was good, as he had to fit in both at home and, later on, at school. Daddy was still giving him more 'lappy time' than was good for him, but was aware that this had to be limited in the coming months to prepare him for the transition to reception year at school.

Sindy and I accompanied Thor, Aaliyah and Caleb to the 'Reception Year' lunch at the school to meet the fellow parents of this year's influx. It was the little ones' first exposure to 'Big School' and, for this epic milestone, they dressed the part in their new school uniforms. They looked very smart, just like real but tiny schoolchildren! We were greeted by the head-mistress and an assortment of teachers, parents, children and PTFA members. The luncheon was yummy and Thor ate large volumes of crisps, sandwiches, biscuits and cakes, as we all did. I ate six sausage rolls and a ham sandwich, and Caleb kept going back for yet another cupcake! It was great to see Ellen there, a fellow parent with a child already in Tara and Amritsar's year. Everyone that I spoke to seemed extremely pleasant, but I had imagined that would be the case. I was hoping to see how our little ones mingled with their new classmates, but there was far too much eating and too little mingling! The little ones enjoyed the day, thank goodness, and are now excited about starting 'Big School' properly in September.

I just want to mention packed lunches, as all parents have to make them. I won't bore you with that age-old debate about what you put in yours, but our children love packed lunches, and I guess it's because they usually signify a trip. That was exactly the reason for Tara and Amritsar's packed lunches one day when they were being packed off to visit a country estate here in The Shires with their classmates. Their last packed lunch for a school trip was a bit of a disaster; their lunch bags fell foul to shoulder straps that were extremely thin and uncomfortable to wear, cutting into the girls' shoulders more and more as the day wore on. So, on this occasion I searched around in the loft and came across some stock from my old 'Glowbag' range. I used to make and promote fluorescent and reflective bags, known as Glowbags. It all started with trying to make road safety look cool, at first with bikers, then I considered cyclists and finally children. Well, the girls were armed with super-comfy-to-wear 'Glowpods' on that day, in a rather fetching fluorescent green and fluorescent orange, and, even if I say so myself, they looked good! Job done!

I think the first thing all of our children drew, once the scribble stage had ended, was a rainbow, and they have continued to draw them ever since. It's funny that, isn't it?

First of all, the colours were applied to their pictures in a random fashion. But recently the colour sequencing has been more specific, radiating from red through the spectrum to violet. All of our children realise the way that the colours morph into the next (red to orange to yellow etc). We haven't progressed on to understanding how the rainbow is made from the splitting of white light (a bit too scientific at this stage), but the children are very aware that each and every colour is just as important as all of the rest!

Now at this point you must realise that I make it my place to be non-political and non-judgmental, but I have to wonder if the LGBTQ community had this in mind when adopting the rainbow as a symbol of unity! So maybe it wasn't all about 'Dorothy' after all. That said, in the wider community, I think that each and every one of us should consider the rainbow and our own unique importance, and that we are, within our own individuality, just as significant as everybody else!

I might just be the only father on the planet that did not post a Facebook pic of 'Father's Day' on the day itself. Rather, I chose to reflect on it here! Daddy and Dadda Love You All.

A poem each, from Amritsar and Tara:

Daddy and Dadda. You are as cuddly as a teddy bear, as hard working as a builder,
as funny as a clown, as cool as a racer,
as amazing as a teacher, as incredible as a chef and as good as an author.
Love from Amritsar xxxxx
(Come to play with me, come to play with me, please, please play with me. Summer time is hear again, come and play with me)

Dadda, Daddy,
you are as tall as a table
as smart as a technician,
as funny as a clown.
Love Tara. X
(You are the best Daddyz in the World)

Do remember the girls are only six years old!

The girl's poetry got me thinking. Remus could sense a change of mood within me, and for some reason I did suddenly feel more sombre. He gently rested his chin on my lap and was glancing upwards, towards me, as I gently stroked his head. I wondered what it was that he sensed? He had also acted strangely earlier in the day on the terrace. You see, we have a 'green wall' covered with ornamental ivy, our rather large grape vine and a sprouting crab apple tree. He was gently pacing the ground, sniffing around quite avidly, almost searching for something that was lost. And then he quietened. I listened, but there was only a silence in the air. I considered the possibility of a red kite hunting in the area. Do you know that bird song freezes when such a competent predator is near? But no, this was different! And then I realised what was wrong.

These last few weeks have seen two very busy, brown-feathered friends at work on our terrace. A mated pair of thrushes firstly built a nest within the ivy, flying inbound with twigs and leaves, and going forth to fetch more. Eggs were laid, and then once hatched, the proud parents had been completely engrossed with the feeding and nurturing of their offspring. Two, maybe three little chicks with very loud, hungry, and urgent sounding chirps had their parents pursuing their own hunting regime. As soon as one parent emerged from the nest after feeding the chicks, the other would appear with a beak full of worms. The frenzy of the chirps erupted again and the cycle would repeat itself again and again.

Today it is silent. I did see a solitary brown song thrush on the lawn, but it did not fly towards the nest hidden beneath the ivy. It just looked around, saw me and then flew away... what happened last night on our terrace? I really do not know, but the veil of silence seemed louder with emptiness now!

There was a Trial Day at school for the little ones, in preparation for joining big school in September. It was the first time in all these years that our not so famous five were all leaving the family home to go to school together, dressed identically in the school's summer uniform; they all looked so smart and grown up - I must admit, it brought a lump to my throat when I lined them up for a photograph. John has been joking that we will have a whopping five per cent of the school's attendance, and he could actually be right! Even so, I don't think I'll be joining the PTFA. anytime soon!

All schools have Sports Day, don't they? Friday was our school's turn; at 8.30 in the morning we got the thumbs up from the head teacher that it would go ahead. It had been a will-it/won't-it situation for days, what with all the recent rain and the local weather forecast. I hate it when the weather is like that. We had hoped for dry as the weather app was inconclusive. And guess what? Come 1 p.m., we arrived to just the merest sprinkling of the wet stuff. Everyone ate their picnics with haste and were then ushered to seats lining the side of the track – the school field had white lines painted to make running lanes. It was nice to see a few friendly faces and meet one or two new ones. The competing school children wore coloured polo shirts depending on which team they were in – red, yellow, green, or blue.

We cheered for 'Team Green' as that was Amritsar's and Tara's team. The whole team did very well and came in at number one – hoorah! We were very proud dads as both girls came first or second in almost all of their races. A major turnaround from last year when they didn't apply the same gusto to their efforts. They both love P.E. nowadays - this might be the reason behind such a good performance. Come 2 p.m. the heavens opened and everyone dived for their brollies. There were over sixty races in all - a constant stream of race after race – and the teachers did a grand job getting everyone in their places quickly in the run up to the rain. Very well-choreographed indeed. Thor did a little track running for himself. And to top it all, Aaliyah also came first in the final run of the day where toddlers and siblings were invited to run the 'toddlers' race'. Thankfully, as the rain grew steadily heavier, the parents run was cancelled. I am remembering last year when John cheated on the egg and spoon race by holding down the egg. Naughty Daddy! Even with that he managed to come last – oh dear...

Thank you so much for the invite from friends Lee and Jess to their oldest son, Angel's birthday party in North London. The soft play party was excellent, as was the later barbeque in the garden. The children loved the face-painting and Lee's dad's home-made sausages were definitely the better of the two that were on offer. I'm really glad about the news on your fourth addition to the family – you'll be overtaking us pretty soon on numbers. Good luck and big hugs you lovely people.

Aaliyah had been very good of late but during the weekend she was back to her old tricks. No, there was no biting involved thankfully, but she did hit Tara in the face at Angel's soft play party and blooded her nose; there was no apology and no regret! Anyhow, she was uncontrollable on the way home in the car. The next morning her foul mood and screams did not dissipate, so I was forced to play my 'Trump' card (nothing to do with the US president, honestly!). I pretended to call Sindy and cancelled her sleepover that night (John was away for the night and I had to be at an event that evening). I then called the fabled 'Mrs Snodgrass' and asked if she could fill in for Sindy and do the sleepover. All of this achieved with Aaliyah listening in. 'Mrs Snodgrass' said that she would be delighted to step in and to finally meet our Aaliyah! My plan was set!

I texted Sindy, who would usually let herself in with her keys, and I asked if she would ring the doorbell instead! Of course, I explained the scenario, and she agreed. Later, I sat with the children, watching television and waiting. The countdown was on – twenty minutes... fifteen minutes... Tara was the most intrigued as she had been asking every half hour when 'Mrs Snodgrass' was arriving! Tara kind of realised that the character was one of fiction, but she was not completely sure. I crumbled a bit earlier and told Tara first, then Amritsar, that I had decided to cancel 'Mrs Snodgrass' (keeping the mystery alive) and Sindy was coming after all. The little ones however were oblivious. Aaliyah was starting to show a certain nervousness, awaiting the sound of the doorbell, glancing anxiously at the window every so often. Ten minutes and counting.

It was 5.15 p.m. when the doorbell rang. Tara, Amritsar, Thor and Caleb were eagerly loitering around the front door in the entrance hall. Tara couldn't contain herself 'Aaliyah, Aaliyah' she was calling 'Mrs Snodgrass is here for you'.

'No, I don't want to come to the door – NO!' Aaliyah shouted, and with a running jump, buried her head beneath the cushions on the sofa.

Tara was giggling as she swung the door open. Caleb and Thor both pushed their way forward, falling on top of each other and landing in a tangle of legs. They picked themselves up, a little dazed. 'Sindy, Sindy' they exclaimed, completely expecting to see Cecelia Snodgrass standing there in her green tweed two-piece suit and spectacles. Amritsar and Tara were laughing and Aaliyah was still hiding in the sofa cushion. When she heard Sindy's voice she slowly raised her head, exhaled, and smiled.

'Did my little joke work Aaliyah – are you now prepared to try a little harder to be a good girl?'

'Yes Dadda, YES,' was her reply. She looked bemused and a little sheepish – no doubt happy that the day's waiting ordeal was over.

Our Crew were asked to do some agreeing for once! We decided to ask them their top things in certain categories - they had to compromise and agree on these results. Hotly and noisily deliberated over dinner they are as follows... (Job well done guys...)

Best TV show: Pocoyo

Best Movie: Chitty Chitty Bang Bang

Best Meal: Broccoli Pesto Pasta (Penne)

Best Confectionary: Marshmallows (Though Thor insisted on candy canes)

Best thing on Toast: Dadda's Jam (of course)

Best subject at School: P.E. (Physical Education)

Best Song: Shake Baby Shake (500) – Lush

Best Game: Hide and Seek

Best colour: Blue, Red, Blue, Orange, Green

Best Thing: A No-brainer really: - Gurney, Kit Koala and Kangy, MiMi, Chicky and Foxy and Doggy (The Children's beloved soft toys)

And not a single Unicorn or the colour pink was mentioned! Well, that's the Children's top ten Besties - for our Crew at least! It certainly made a riot of dinnertime!

Shouting was heard so I ventured up to the top floor to see what all of the fuss was about! Tara had trapped her arm at the wall-side of her bed. It was stretched into the abyss that lay at the back of her bottom bunk! As I rushed through the boy's room, Caleb lay silent - Little Mr Sleepy was clearly counting lambs and dancing with dreams. Thor on the other hand jumped to attention, 'Come on Dadda, come on – let's free Tara.' He skipped alongside me and we entered the girl's room. Tara was still wailing, 'Help me Dadda, my arm is trapped'. I pulled the bed from the wall with a little help from Aaliyah and Amritsar, and I investigated the pile of books that lay before me. Tara had only dropped one, the reason for her cries for help, but there lay a small library of children's fiction. Thor was in there first. 'This one's mine,' he shrieked. And then Aaliyah joined in, 'I'm having this one,' she shouted. Both of them grabbed book after book until, finally, the remains of the booty were shared between them.

Wouldn't you know it! We'd been planning and looking forward to it for weeks: a twenty-four-hour mini holiday near Bude, North Cornwall. We arrived on Britain's hottest day in years. And guess what? In Bude it was 17 degrees centigrade, foggy and cold. At home it was 32 degrees centigrade and brilliant sunshine!

This was supposed to be a trial night for our two-week break in August, but I felt a certain dismay. Was it really worth the four hours' drive, during which we were repeatedly being asked 'Are we there yet?'

It was chilly and grey when we arrived, but rest assured, we did not let it dissuade us from ice creams by the sea! Four chocolate and one vanilla cone for the not so famous five, enjoyed on round rustic picnic benches outside the café next to the beach. The children changed into their swimming togs – cute old-fashioned one-piece affairs, with stripes, and little life jackets over, just in case – and went to explore rockpools. They ran and splashed, laughed and sat in the water, and found tiny little creatures swimming in the shallows. Luckily, we'd remembered towels this time, because there was a chill breeze and they cooled down fairly quickly, so we dried them off, packed everything up, and headed to our accommodation.

Just when you thought you had passed a hurdle – you realised that you hadn't. There were screams for the rest of the day with the little ones, and all of their behaviour showed its darker side at several flash points during the afternoon. We had two 'Thinking Chairs' on the go at one point, and both Aaliyah and Caleb sat there looking shame faced. Amritsar and Tara on the other hand had been model students.

While we watched the children playing in the garden before bedtime, the sun finally broke through the clouds and I could feel the warmth of it on my face. It was quite hot, and it was at that point that we realised we'd forgotten to pack our Panama hats! Drat! Something always gets forgotten! The clouds soon covered the sun again, the temperature dipped, and it was time to go inside.

By the time the children were in bed and we'd had our grown-up's dinner, John and I sat in the garden of the beach house with a well-deserved glass of white wine, looking out across the beach and the Atlantic Ocean just as the sun was setting. We'd be heading home again tomorrow, our mini-holiday at an end. Had it been a relaxing getaway? Probably not – but had we confirmed our two-week summer holiday in North Cornwall? Yes, two weeks of full-on holiday mayhem to look forward to!

On the journey home the children were tired and fairly subdued, for the most part, but it got a bit lively somewhere around Bristol, town of my birth. Aaliyah was screeching profusely behind me, Daddy was beginning to lose his temper, and I had to raise my voice several times. Dadda started to get 'one of his heads' – oh dear! Roll on August – and don't forget to pack the paracetamol!

The very wet month we've just witnessed reminded me of the harvest last year.

We'd had two days of constant rain and drizzle, and as soon as it was dry, I rushed out to harvest the last twenty percent of our 'Concord' grape vine. It had been a bumper year due to the phenomenal amount of sunshine and heat and I'd already managed to pick most of it. On the other hand, the Apple harvest from the trees in the kitchen garden was appalling. I wanted to simply juice the remainder of the grapes and then planned to freeze it for jamming at another time. If the provisions cupboard could talk, it would say, 'Not another Grape Jelly, I'm so full up!'.

There were a few moldy bunches which I discarded, but I think I just about caught the rest of the crop before it was doomed. I immersed them in a sink full of water, not only to clean them but also to rid them of earwigs, which love to make their homes inside these sweet, seeded vine fruits.

Juicing grapes is a slow process. The first year that I attempted to juice our first crop of grapes, in my pure ignorance, I spent two hours trying to pass them through a muslin bag. Well, a white pillow case actually. It took absolutely hours to release the juice! This year's bumper crop of grapes would have easily taken a couple of days if I'd done it that way. Anyhow, this year I cropped the vine in four stages. The total weight of grapes was in excess of twelve kilograms. Without child labour this year (see below), I washed the black grapes and filled the very large saucepan I use for jamming, then squeezed like mad with my hands. Once the juice was released, I kept topping up the pan until seventy percent full, then to help release more juice I heated until boiling. Then with my trusty new sieve (I've gone through three so far this year!) I scooped out the pith and seeds and pressed firmly on the mixture with a spoon so that the final juice was released. (I discard the pith.) Once boiled and the scum is skimmed, you have pasteurised juice that is fit to make perfect 'Grape Jelly'.

I thought back to the previous September when we harvested early. It was a weekend and the weather was mild. Not sure how sunny it was, but it must have been fairly warm because I remember John and I had a Pimm's and lemonade poured. All five little ones had their swimming costumes on. We had been playing 'The water slide' - don't mix up 'water sliding' with 'water boarding'! We put down a ten-meter strip of black tarpaulin and someone held the hosepipe at the top of the children's green slide. The children love it, so much screaming and shouting and above all sliding. And it's competitive too.

I've gone off focus - back to the grape vine and child labour! Secateurs in hand and the children's small paddling pool beside me, I was pruning away and throwing the bunches of grapes directly into the pool. It wasn't long before Tara came running up screaming, 'Aaliyah hit me, Aaliyah hit me!' Then she saw what I was doing. The vine was fifty percent done and the pool was filling up slowly. Tara didn't give it a second though. She jumped in and started squishing with her feet shouting out, 'Ritza, Ritza,' to Amritsar, 'come here it's fun'.

Within minutes the others were over to investigate. First Amritsar, and then Thor, joined Tara in the paddling pool, both also jumping up and down, laughing and screaming. 'It's squishy Dadda it's squishy,' Thor screamed, and fists clenched tight, he stamped harder, one foot after the other. Aaliyah and Caleb were bemused, sitting with Daddy at the table on the terrace, under the parasol. Daddy raised his Pimm's and lemonade and said, 'Cheers'. I continued pruning and throwing in the bunches...

Chapter Nine and A Half

Television Stars!

"Shoot for the moon. Even if you miss, you'll land among the stars."
— Les Brown

We had quite an exciting time of it this summer, having been approached by a television company regarding a new Parenting show, a competition type thing. Here's what happened...

The television company contacted me through Instagram in early May. After several emails back and forth, we were interviewed on Facetime - and they liked us! The following Sunday they came out to us to do a provisional montage of family scenes, and they interviewed us on our parenting style. Or lack of maybe! We settled on 'Organised Chaos', which pretty much sums up having five children aged between three and six. We met a cameraman/researcher called Kieron, and Ciara the casting producer. Both young, trendy, and chatty - cool kids! They loved us!

The show is going to be called 'Britain's Best Parent'. It will consist of four episodes showing each set of parents, in their own homes, 'parenting' the other children in the show; the fifth episode will be the final where a studio audience will decide on the winner. The day of the studio filming in London will be set in late July/early August and the program is due to be aired in September or October 2019 on primetime Channel 4.

There were lots of forms to fill in: for licenses for the girls to attend the other houses, a form for the local authorities, there were school absence forms, medical questionnaires for all of the children and us for insurance etc, plus a DBS check on both John and me. We even had an interview with 'Howey' a third-party psychologist, who talked with us to make sure we were okay with possible scenarios - you know, daytime TV interviews, or negative articles in the Daily Mail and on social media, that sort of thing.

The first shoot here was our trailer for Channel 4, and I think that everyone was excited. Kosta was the director, and Sam seconded him, picking angles and parts of the house that would be used on our main day. John knows that a high profile equals possible book sales, so he's been brilliant for coming onboard. I was initially a little nervous with the camera, but Kosta was very friendly, experienced at putting people at ease, and I was soon relaxed and spontaneous.

The days of filming were moved about a bit but the day out in the Cotswolds, for the girls to spend the day with another set of parents, fell on a Sunday, and they put us up in a hotel in West Swindon. On the day, Tara and Amritsar were brilliant. Inquisitive, not too shy - both excited. I quite honestly didn't know what to think. 'Why am I doing this?' I asked myself. I'm certainly not a pushy parent, but I decided it was definitely the right thing to get involved in as the girls were really happy to participate in the experience.

Driving up to the other contributor's house felt a bit surreal, and there were lots of questions about the day ahead. They filmed the drop off (twice). The girls looked very excited by this point and the other parents came over well. They had three daughters. In the taxi back to the hotel where John was waiting with the little ones, I knew the girls would have a great time. We spent the day at the hotel. Had lunch and used the rather crowded hotel swimming pool. Thor was very naughty at the restaurant, shouting and trying to run away from the table. Feet kicking at one point. Mind you Aaliyah's and Caleb's behaviours weren't much better. At 3.30 p.m. we all drove to the house to collect the girls. It was just me who did the bit for the camera, to pick up the girls. They emerged looking as if they'd had a good day, and I saw one of the other parents who was there to pick up his son. The TV crew kept us apart obviously, so we will no doubt be more spontaneous on the parent's meet-up day in London.

The following Wednesday we were in London for the other drop off. Sindy drove us to the station after school and we took a train up. Yes, the girls were ecstatic to be travelling on a train. We stayed in West London and took a taxi to the other house at 5.45 a.m. the next morning. All stage managed, more questions and responses to the scenario. They filmed my drop off. The girls were again excited, and at 3.30 p.m. I returned and collected them. They filmed me collecting them and that was that! We took a taxi to Paddington - Amritsar had a meltdown at the station when I said that the Paddington bears were too expensive to buy. Thirty quid each for a Paddington Bear soft toy, and I would've had to buy two! We sat on a bench in the station and calmed down before boarding the train.

The main filming for us happened during the May bank holiday at our house, and it was manic from the start. Filming started early; the crew arrived about 6 a.m. as planned, so we were ship-shape and Bristol-fashion by 5.30 a.m. The crew consisted of Emma, Sam the cameraman, two sound engineers, two chaperones for the two visiting children, a runner, someone on his computer screen - not sure what he was doing - and the Executive Producer, Jeremy. Oh, and two visiting children with the two separate drop offs. The filming was endless!

The little ones acted much like any other weekend morning - a bit screamy and demanding. Tara and Amritsar were more aware of what was in store. They didn't talk much about their days with the other families, but small things emerged, like 'Lolly's' dad was a mad inventor! Little things like that. We had recently watched Chitty Chitty Bang Bang as a family and my mind could only wonder! Lolly (Lauren) was a nine-year-old girl and daughter of said 'inventor' and Lewis was the other chap who joined us for the day. His family were Asian/Chinese, so I immediately knew they were probably very organised and, without a doubt, had a stricter environment than ours. He was eight years old.

Once everything was set up on the production front and the crew were filming, after we did the drop off and the children were settled, I got out seven t-shirts of various colours. I'm not particularly 'I'm here, I'm queer - get used to it!' as you may have noticed, but our day was just a little bit 'Rainbow'. The children dressed in the sequence of colours within the rainbow. I told them all that I had chosen the rainbow, firstly as all children love rainbows, but most importantly because every single colour is just as 'Important' as all the others!!! They chose their favourite colours and, luckily, they were all different! Lolly chose violet, and Amritsar was blue. Next was Lewis, he chose that often-overlooked colour indigo; Caleb chose his beloved green, Aaliyah was yellow, Thor was orange and Tara was red.

We had carefully planned activities for the day. First of all, we did 'Cereal Box Crowns'. I cut the zig-zags from the flattened boxes with ease as we up-cycle the recycling and make crowns every now and again. This time I spent the night before covering the branding with large white sticky labels. No intrusive advertising, remember! We embellished them with sticky gems and colouring pens. I then crowned each of the children. They all seemed to be getting on well...

I tried to arrange them all on the stairs in the order of the colours of the rainbow, but that proved impossible to organise, so I sat them on the sofa in perfect sequence, and welcomed Princess Violet and Prince Indigo to our crew.

Our next activity was in the garden. It was a little overcast, but warm. The children were going to help me do some weeding, and then they were going to plant some sunflower seeds. All fairly straightforward stuff. Lolly had removed her violet tee shirt in favour of the hoody that she had arrived in. I wasn't worried about it really, but was concerned that she was feeling okay! She assured me that she was, so I let it drop. They did some good weeding in the large pots containing courgettes, tomatoes and pepper plants. Lots of small weeds were removed and the small piles were put on top of our big pile for composting.

Then Lewis climbed onto an old drystone wall that separates the upper and lower terraces. I asked him if he could get down, but he was so happy he was oblivious to my request. He was clearly having a great time of it all. I rose my voice a little saying that he was standing on a 'Snakes Nest' and should probably move away. He really was jumping up and down on the nest that contained maybe twenty various sizes of grass snakes coming out of hibernation. Emma, the director, thought that I was using an imaginary threat to settle him down! He jumped off, and out of danger from falling the one metre plus drop the other side of the wall, not really considering the threat of meeting an angry, slithering reptile. Later in the day in conversation, I confirmed to Emma that 'Yes, it was a real nest of snakes!'

We moved on, activity wise, to the large rainbow Piñata. The TV company had done the 'Risk Assessment' form and allowed it, though when I handed the large bamboo stick to Lolly, I was more than slightly shocked by the ferocity of her swinging and shaking of the stick. Remember, our guys are all under six, and a nine-year-old has a lot more strength. I was running around raggedly, keeping the little ones out of harm's way. Lewis was the next to have a go and, again, being eight years old, he was a lot stronger! I hadn't really thought through the possible dangers of trying to beat a hard cardboard-and-tissue rainbow! Silly Dadda!

Our crew all tried; we laughed a lot and I noticed that Lolly was finally happy and in a much better place. Thor's and Aaliyah's swings were paramount to insanity, so I retired the small ones and they sat it out with Daddy. I still had to duck and dive with the bigger four children though. Twenty minutes in and the Piñata still hung tight with sweets. Amritsar and Tara sat back to leave Lolly and Lewis to do their thing. Finally, Lolly won the battle and sweets sprung a plenty, followed by Lewis who demolished the other side of the rainbow. Whilst all this was going on Thor, who is a real coveter of stuff, was diving in and out of the danger zone picking up the fallen tissue paper. Completely bonkers in its entirety, but I guessed it would make good TV. When I told everybody that we would have the sweets after lunch, that didn't go down well at all – who tells children that (after a Piñata) they would have to wait for their well-earned sweets until after lunch? And, to add insult to injury, that everyone would be sharing them evenly!

We moved on to lunch with our family favourite, 'Chips'n'Choices'. I made deep-fried torn potatoes and whirled around the busy kitchen table offering a myriad of leftovers. There was cottage pie, pasta bolognaise, cooked sausages, chicken Rendang, and chilli con carne. They all screamed for bolognaise, only two portions left, so a compromise was made. Emma was pointing her camera everywhere, jumping around, beaming with a huge smile constantly, as chatty as can be! To be honest, her enthusiasm was quite tiring!

After lunch, the two chaperones for the visiting children helped them into their swimwear, and we got our not so famous five into theirs. It was time for the 'Slip and Slide' or, simply, the water slide, not to be mistaken for 'Water Boarding'! This event was the high point really. The screams, shouts, laughs - and more screams of pure delight - were constant. The green slide was laid out with a four-metre black tarpaulin at the bottom, and the garden hose was held at the top of the slide by daddy, then later, Thor, who screamed and screamed and laughed lots.

Lewis decided to sneak off and go tree climbing up the ancient, oversized rhododendron bushes. I couldn't believe it when I looked up and there he was shouting from the top of the branches. It seems that he had limited freedoms back at home, coming from a fairly regimented, Chinese family, so he was taking every opportunity to have as good a time as he possibly could whilst surrounded by a bunch of children all going crazy. Lolly also was really happy at this point and she did the best slip and slide; I guess it was due to the fact that she was much larger in size than the others, being that she was nine-years-old. I guess when it comes to velocity on water, mass has to be considered!

The day for the children ended at around 4 p.m. At this point I guessed that if the upcoming studio audience were voting on 'Britain's Best Parents' for having the most fun, we would have been clear winners. But the day filming in 'The Studio' would come about six weeks later. The logistics of this kind of programming, fitting in with the children, parents' schedules, weekends, availability of the crew, all depends on precise planning from the producers.

Our day was not yet over. John and I changed clothes and Emma, the director, and Sam, the other cameraman, sat us on chairs in the living room. The children kept running in but Sindy, our nanny, corralled them all into the kitchen and did some drawing with them, and later made sandwiches for their dinner. The producer and excess staff all slowly cleared out leaving just one runner with Emma and Sam. So, there were sporadic goodbyes every now and then, but you know those cameras are running all of the time, so they got what they wanted plus a fair amount more.

The interview on our unique parenting style was communicated well. We both said how we saw benefit from certain chaos that leads to decision making, and the social implications of what was being considered. Emma told us 'You guys really owned that,' so we were upbeat about the day's events, though I am sure she said that to absolutely everybody. Finally, they left, taking the rest of their equipment with them. Sindy, after having put our crew up to bed, popped her head around the door to ask us how the interview went. 'Who knows and who cares?' was my reply. John looked a little more sombre 'I hope we don't win this bloody thing - I have a business to run!' was his reply. We all laughed, and Sindy departed. We had a few well-deserved glasses of wine that night.

The summer was flying by and soon enough the Studio date was upon us. John and I met in London and were picked up by an Addison Lee taxi to take us to the studio somewhere in Wapping, East London. We met Ciara and the girl from the office, Chanele, who had organised trains, taxis etc. Nice to finally put a face to a name. We were ushered into a small dressing room and wardrobe made some choices with the small collection of clothes that we had brought with us in a holdall. Then makeup did their thing. We saw Howie, the psychologist that we had met earlier; he said hello and lovely to see you, and then goodbye, as he was leaving. He told us that the other psychologist we would be meeting was also great, and left.

After the chat with the other psychologist, we met up with Kosta again, and we did some shots of us arriving, then repeat shots of us looking in a certain direction, then another. They do like to prepare for all eventualities in this type of show. There were then a few promotional pictures taken of John and me by a professional photographer with his state-of-the-art Canon super camera thingy. Job done. Time to eat! We had a meal of something that looked very Vegan and healthy, lots of green, pulses and beans. No, come to think of it, there was a bit of chicken in there somewhere, I recall.

They were filming all four studio elements for all four episodes on the same day, so they must have had a complete logistical nightmare to contend with. It was difficult enough making sure that we didn't bump into the other parents from our episode, Becky and Ben, and Richard and Emily. They were all very nice people and their children were all amazing.

It was finally time for our episode to be filmed. Anita Rani, from Countryfile fame, was compering the show. She was great – very chatty and likeable. The studio audience was from a cross section of society, we could only wait and see. I didn't feel at all anxious but, to be honest, I did feel a little awkward. John was great and said what he thought of the other parenting styles with relative ease. I, on the other hand, was a little more subdued; I don't remember being overly chatty, just made a few comments - one had everyone in stitches - and I did make quite a few intrigued, amused, and even amazed looks for the camera. We can't wait to see the show when it finally airs on Channel 4.

Sadly, we did not go through to the final. The audience voted through Becky and Ben, the 'Home Schooling' family. It really was very sweet how Becky shed a few tears and released some emotion as to the occasional bigotry she has experienced down to the fact that they chose home schooling as a way of life. It is all about acceptance really isn't it? And that is one of the reasons that I chose to 'Be on a Show' – if people see how normal our family life is, as crazy and whacky, loving and fun - just how normal it is; there really is nothing to fear or be uncomfortable with when you see a couple of loving Dads with five amazing beautiful children. Family comes in all shapes and forms, not just a mummy and a daddy.

Chapter Ten
July

"That's one small step for a man, one giant leap for mankind"
— Neil Armstrong

For Aaliyah and Caleb's fourth birthday I really went to town with the cake; it was the biggest one I'd ever made and had four – yes, four! – layers as opposed to my usual three. The sponges were lavishly spread between each layer with home-made ganache and blackcurrant jelly, and not just any home-made blackcurrant jelly, but made from our own home-grown blackcurrants! There was a thick layer of fudge icing, and four candles stood to attention, awaiting their turn to shine.

Sindy's sister, Sally, had given costumes to the twins; Aaliyah's was a Unicorn, complete with several shades of sparkly pink netting in the skirt, and a unicorn-horned hat; she was twirling and dancing, and rejoicing in being a unicorn. Caleb's was Cat Boy; a superhero cat, with a blue stripy onesie and a mask; he insisted on hiding behind furniture, then creeping up on us, pouncing and grabbing our legs. They were delighted with themselves and wore the costumes all day.

The sun shone brightly and it truly felt like summer was just around the corner; perfect for an outdoor birthday party. Thirty children, with their respective parents in tow, turned up at the appointed time clutching presents and cards; there were lots of hello's and children jumping up and down with excitement, and they were very soon running around the garden shrieking (the children, not the parents)! Gracie and Remus quite sensibly hid on the sofa in the living room, away from the many grabby little hands. Sindy's preparations for the party were amazing and she put together a fabulous buffet that was demolished in no time by both adults and children. Everyone seemed to have an amazing time, and I think that was particularly due to having a very formidable children's entertainer for two of the three hours. I'm happy to report that the party began and finished well with no mishaps or major meltdowns!

It had been a long day, but before we all retired for the night, happy and sleepy, everything was tidied away, the dishwasher loaded, and dozens of gifts were neatly stacked onto the garden bench on the terrace, to be investigated the next day. I don't like to come down in the mornings to find a messy kitchen or untidy house, so I was satisfied all was as it should be when I made my way upstairs.

I slept extremely well, but when I arose the following morning my dreamy sleep was soon forgotten. John had allowed the children to play in the garden before I woke, and the sight that greeted me on the terrace made my heart sink. Instead of a bench neatly stacked with birthday gifts, the seat was empty, wrapping paper and gift bags were scattered the length and breadth of the terrace, boxes were torn open, and the contents strewn without care.

But that was just the beginning! I managed to tidy up as the day progressed, again and again, in different areas, over and over, but it was like a landslide, and I felt I was fighting completely against the laws of nature and physics. Puzzles had been opened and their contents strewn to the wind. Games with many plastic pieces, also thrown to the winds. A plastic doll lay there, the clothing everywhere, her head completely removed – decapitated and lifeless. It seemed that the children were out of control, and telling them to stop making a mess was hopeless – it fell on deaf ears. By 1 p.m. I had had enough and escaped to the bedroom for an hour's respite. The tranquillity of the room was blissful and I closed my ears to the distant shrieks and calls that I could hear downstairs. It was a much needed and appreciated break from the bedlam, but I knew it was only temporary.

What I returned to was a house completely trashed... whoever gave the sticky mosaic craft gift, well - I would very much like to know your name as I will gladly reciprocate in good time! The sticky mosaics were everywhere I looked and I was reminded of the forensic tidy and clean up after the kinetic sand incident!

Later, when John had managed, with difficulty, to get them into their jimjams, I locked myself in our bedroom, refusing to see anyone or say goodnight to any of them, despite the knockings on the door, and the shouts of 'Dadda, Dadda...'. I felt like a broken man. I didn't want to venture back to the ground floor due to the amount of mess, destruction, and chaos that still remained there. I completely gave up and preferred not to leave the relative sanctity of my bedroom. I could only rejoice in the knowledge that that was the last birthday party in our immediate family for the next six months. Or ever!

Thankfully, the following day was a huge improvement on the shenanigans of the previous day; the children frolicked happily in the garden and the sun shone warmly while they played and ran, and expended the huge amount of energy that they seem to generate in vast amounts. Summer had finally arrived in The Shires.

When I was stranded in Mumbai, some six years ago, I became unfit and very depressed. This was around the time I lost a lot of weight due to the unforeseen circumstances surrounding my coming home with the girls and I ended up going on a hunger strike. I was, essentially, a prisoner on the

Indian sub-continent, unable to leave with our daughters as they needed an exit visa. I needed one too as I had outstayed my six-month tourist visa due to the fact that I could not be parted from our babies, Amritsar and Tara. I had to apply for a temporary visa every week in order to stay in India, and I would also have to wait for and apply for my own 'Exit Visa' in order to return home (whilst also having to pay the Indian authorities a hefty fine!).

Our nannies, Manju and Nikki, threatened to leave if I didn't start to eat again, and the Delhi-based female lawyer, who was trying to represent our case to the authorities, could only say to me, 'Oh, Mr Andrew, going without food here in India has no merit! Many people live here with hunger, what makes you so special'? Nobody was really any the wiser regarding my hunger strike, so I reluctantly began to consume food again, and I also began a regime of light exercise. I called it bed'ercise as it was mostly me stretching and flexing whilst lying on the bed in the apartment.

And now, thinking about it, I realise that I have never actually admitted to occasional exercise! I really don't know why I haven't said anything, but I've kept up those light workouts for all this time. From the initial twenty repetitions of each individual exercise, it settled on fifty of each. I'm not bulked out, just feeling fitter on a muscular level.

Anyway, I recently met up with a personal trainer, Adam. I hoped to be seeing him twice a week initially to help fine-tune my workouts and, hopefully, feel that much fitter and overall healthier as a result. I'm really glad I have made the commitment and will of course keep you updated...

During the week, what with school and preschool and Sindy's calm and organised structure, we generally have a smooth time of it and the days pass fairly peacefully. You may have sussed that our major breakdowns usually happen at the weekend when Daddy is here, as they all play up for Daddy, competing for his attention as they see far less of him than they do of me. One mid-week night however, the moment that Sindy headed home, Amritsar's screams could be heard shouting for Gurney, her white and green favourite teddy bear. I called up that she could come down and I would retrieve him from the kitchen. She met me at the bottom of the stairs, and I handed over her overly-loved, limp and squashed little bear, and within seconds Tara also appeared, popping her head around the balustrade on the mid landing. As she descended, so did Thor; down they strolled, followed by Aaliyah and finally, Caleb. Sindy had been gone for less than five minutes!

Thor was chat, chat, chat, even while Amritsar and I had a hug, and then a 'kiss and hug' for Aaliyah, then Tara and Caleb. 'Come on guys,' I exclaimed. 'You really need to head back up.' Thor was still chat, chat, chat. Amritsar headed back up the stairs (clutching Gurney to her chest) as did the others, all bar Thor, who was still chat, chat, chat.

He finally concluded his little chat with 'I love you Dadda, and thank you for our little chat!'

And while I remember, an unreported milestone from a couple of weeks back. Whilst visiting a friend's home Thor, being a bit taller than a few months ago, asked if he could do the 'boys grown-up pee pee'? 'I don't see why not' I exclaimed! And so, he did!

And there we have it, one extremely proud little boy took his first steps to becoming a 'big boy'. He was so very proud of himself. As we were of him.

A lot of parenting is about experiencing the 'first time' for everything, isn't it? There are so many moments to remember and still so many to come...

One Saturday saw me alone with the children as John was in Dublin for the day to be with his mum and sisters. Our day had its ups and downs. We started with a fairly sombre tone as there was no Daddy to play up to, and all remained calm for most of the morning. We played a game with one of the twin's birthday presents, a sort of wooden hoopla-type set up; rope rings were thrown to land on hooks, and scores added up. I'd only turned my back for one dratted moment when MiMi became impaled on one of the hooks! Nobody owned up, and neither did they a short time later when MiMi disappeared, only to be found submerged in a bucket of water by the back door! I managed to retrieve him from a screaming Thor and put him in the washing machine for an eco-wash and spin. He came out so much fresher than he had been, and Thor hung on to him tightly for the rest of the day.

After a pasta lunch, screen time was allowed, and a trancelike state was enjoyed for maybe two hours. And then came the spontaneous 'Crazy Kids' outbreak of the screaming run-around-the-sofa for an hour or so. Strangely, suspiciously, they settled into bed without bother, no doubt due to the sheer exhaustion of their earlier antics. I fully expected them to appear downstairs at some point, but they never did!

John arrived home around 9.30 p.m. and dinner was a simple affair of dressed crab on sourdough toast. If I have learnt anything in the last couple of years – it is that it's fine to purchase pre-picked crab meat! I used to always pick my own, buying whole frozen or fresh Cromer Crabs and working up a sweat to extract every morsel of meat! Well, you live and learn, don't you?

Sunday began with an early rise and the shouts of 'Can we build the swimming pool; can we build the swimming pool'? Thank you to our relations in Ireland for the gift of a non-inflatable pool. We have had a pool every summer for the last three years, usually a large inflatable one which gets broken before the autumnal fall. Hopefully, since this one isn't inflatable, and has rigid sides, it should last the whole summer.

John gave in after a couple of hours and set about the mammoth task of building the all-important pool. It took hours to fill, and the not so famous five became a little impatient, getting changed into swimming togs and climbing in when it was only half full. While the older four were in and out, playing with water toys and splashing each other, Caleb took some considerable time getting into the water; first a hand, then a toe, was dipped in, and quickly removed. Then one leg while he balanced on the little step, and eventually all of him was in. Aaliyah held tight to her unicorn-horn hat from her birthday costume, while Amritsar teased the little ones with the hose spray that we were using to fill the pool. They were all loving it, giggling and chasing and splashing each other, so here's to lots of summer fun and frolics.

Wow – it was warm in the UK, and indeed the heat was shared all over Europe. In the next days we had a unified weather front with all of our European neighbours, though you might be aware that we were about to leave the political unity that was once Europe! As you know I make it my place not to comment on politics. Anyhow, on that specific day, we had a new prime minister. NO COMMENT!

What with all the talk this July of the 50th anniversary of the lunar landings, plus the partial lunar eclipse here in the U.K. I realised I had been remiss in not mentioning the 'Full Moon' for a while! I think that with last month's subscription to 'Kindle Unlimited' (and the month prior) prohibiting the electronic publication of 'Eighteen Moons' on any platform other than Amazon, I decided not to continue with the subscription from early August. The exercise of joining Kindle Select had found 'Eighteen Moons' an additional 500+ readers, and I suppose that can't be a bad thing. And for you guys, please don't forget that the paperback and eBook version of the story is still available through your Amazon account, simply by searching 'Eighteen Moons'.

This is an interesting time. These past twelve months have taken us from being a fairly chaotic bunch of little people, post baby and toddler stage, to a family of five young children (now between the ages of four and six) having begun or about to take their 'School Years' Experience'. This coming chapter in their lives will ultimately help define them all and begin to fine-tune their futures as they prepare to fly a little way from the nest.

The mated pair of thrushes that had abandoned their nest last month had been busy! About three weeks ago they returned and started to spruce up the nest hidden within the ivy and grapevine on our 'green wall'. Seemingly no expense was spared on the interior decor front – they both worked hard to reinforce the structure and wings were often heard a-flapping in order to create an internal space that would accommodate a new brood. There was some silence for a while, and then the chirp, chirp, chirp of tiny chicks could be heard once again.

I was so filled with happiness that these committed feathered neighbours were once more blessed with the chance of being a family. Sitting on our terrace with my early morning cup of coffee, I felt in awe as I watched a small storm of flying ants. They came, seemingly out of nowhere, to dance the day away, always on a hot day. Then one of the thrushes came close - it felt a little unreal as this feathered couple are usually quite aloof and not particularly keen on coming too close to us humans. But one of the thrushes came within a metre of me several times, and sounded a strange vocal note, very unlike any bird sound that I have ever heard. It flitted around and around, transporting beak-fulls of these little insects again and again, up to the nest, then back for more. The chick's chirps erupted feverishly on every single journey.

The experience was mesmerising – I felt the undemanding gift of nature and its true relationship with family. We are all born with 'need' aren't we? But nurture alongside nature can turn that need into something so much more constructive. And that is selfless want; I remember the time when John and I decided to become a family! I think we managed our expectations and experience well, though a certain amount of grief and adversity prevailed. Pride is what we feel for our children, and of our previous achievements, in becoming the family that we are today.

Our first week of the school holidays had almost passed. The start of the week saw me postpone my initial workout with the personal trainer until next week. The children had been enjoying the outdoors; even with the heatwave there has been some fun and games in the pool. Thank goodness we thought to erect the gazebo over the pool, to give some much-needed shade as the sun was beating down unmercifully.

Sadly, John had gone back to Dublin for a couple of days as his mother was extremely unwell at that point and I wished her well; the children had made her pictures and gifts which

John had taken with him. Our nanny took them all out to Thatcham Lake to feed the ducks and I enjoyed a small respite before lunch. Remus was barking sporadically with every tiny sound that he heard. He is always a little sensitive and when waiting for the children to return from school or a trip and he listens intently for the slightest sound that might be them! Gracie is much more laid back and can usually be found lolloping on the sofa.

Later, all five children and I hid on the terrace in order to spot the Thrush and hear the chirps of the chicks. We sat at the table for five minutes under the parasol, quietly hiding, waiting for the thrush to return from its forage with a beak full of worms. Tara decided that we all needed to be camouflaged, so she and Thor darted back inside to grab hoodies, Barbour jackets and M65 jackets to swaddle everyone in. It was already very hot! As we sat there waiting rather uncomfortably, Thor decided that MiMi (his much beloved bear) was too hot, so he headed back inside, just as the thrush arrived and the chicks erupted into their feeding frenzy. 'I'm missing it – I'm missing it,' he screamed, and ran back outside. Well, we waited a little more and saw the thrush return a second time, and then Aaliyah got bored so we all returned inside to the relative cool of the living room.

I was completely exhausted from a busy yet fun weekend. John finally arrived home from his gruelling journey that is the dratted Sunday afternoon flight from Dublin to London Heathrow. Thank you, Air Lingus, (British Airways), for the fourth delayed flight in a row, on this very popular route at the most desired time of the day!

The last week of July was a busy time, what with the children being children and just me to corral them and manage our time of arts, crafts and play. Lots of screams and laughs and plenty of debate with Thor and Aaliyah. Caleb, a boy of little words, was still using the power of pure scream to deliver himself, so Dadda did have to say that he was getting 'one of his heads' a couple of times, quickly followed by Thor agreeing that he was getting a headache also. He raised his tone and said, 'Please Caleb (or Aaliyah), you must be a little quieter as my head is hurting a little bit'. He does make me smile.

Aaliyah's fingers in her mouth is something that I have held back on drawing too much attention to in the past, as I believe that we all went through that stage in our earlier years. Of our crew, Tara spent some time managing the 'wrinkly finger syndrome'. Though with regards to Aaliyah, many of our family photos going back to her very early days show her with the middle and index fingers of her right hand firmly in her mouth! We've talked about it a lot in the past couple of weeks and she is aware that she must try a bit harder to stop it in the weeks leading up to the start of 'Big School'.

Anyhow, we came to a compromise; she knows that there is a lotion available from the chemist that helps to quell the habit, but we settled on the wearing of a single woollen glove. She was very good and kept it on for the majority of the day. All in all, she did not deposit the fingers of her gloved right hand into her mouth. Well done, Aaliyah.

But I do have one thing to add, and that is, like me, she shows signs of being ambidextrous, which meant she was quite confident to plug her left hand in when she felt needy enough for the comfort of sucking fingers. As a matter of fact, I always lay her spoon or fork on the left-hand side every breakfast, lunch and dinner! Like me she mostly uses her right hand but has the capacity to use her left hand in just the same way. I do hope her new school do not try to make her choose when she starts in September. I can actually write with my left hand in reverse to what my right hand is writing if I practice for a few minutes. Perfect symmetry with reverse wording or shapes and patterns come to think of it. I remember that it used to come in handy when I worked in design before the onset of 'Family Life'. I often found myself doing totally different jobs with each of my hands!

I noted about six months back that, ever since the girls started preschool, the one constant in my life had been a very snotty nose, excessive sneezing, and coughing aplenty. And when they left preschool the little ones started there, and have been there these last two years. Well, this disgusting cold has constantly prevailed. It's not just the wiping of the children's noses week in and week out, but I have caught every single cold that has been brought home! I wash my hands some forty times a day; however, with the children sharing toys at preschool - from mouth to hand to mouth - the viruses prevail.

Funny, however, that the moment Amritsar and Tara went to 'Big School', they have not brought home a single cold! Another amazing fact is that they have not once ever picked up one of these new colds; they have clearly developed great immunity. I look forward to a future life without sneezing and coughing on a daily basis as the accepted norm.

For a few days the sunshine disappeared and the weather really sucked! The rain, wind, and more rain, were more akin to my memories of school summer holidays 'back in the day'; back then we were allowed so many more freedoms than children have today. It seemed a much safer time somehow, and we were allowed out to play from a younger age, with neighbouring children or siblings. We played in the local park or even in the street, as there were fewer cars on the roads, but if it was raining, we were stuck indoors! I suppose it was just as well we had all that outdoor freedom as only having three television channels that didn't show any programmes until at least teatime - really dismal! I remember on the children's holidays, the BBC would rerun rubbish old shows, even the likes of the ancient 1930's Flash Gordon, and movies like 'Beau Geste'! What was that all about? I remember really hating the summer rain. If you couldn't go out to play there really was very little to do. I think today's options are a lot more stimulating.

Well, I must add that our Kindle 7's were on overdrive during the wet and windy spell. The children are not allowed them before midday and even then, we do monitor the amount of usage. Who invented 'Crossy Road'? The children love that game. Though I am not sure that I like the addictive nature of 'candy crush' as Amritsar has just become very upset that she cannot progress through a level. Had I already said, this weather really sucks? Oh, the thought of the Mediterranean!

Taste of North Africa

Every few weeks I find myself desiring something spicy, yet mild and warming! The fragrance - a little less Thai, and its hit - a little less Indian within its complexity of layers. The perfect flavour for this kind of mood would be the intoxicating aroma of a Moroccan Bazaar, that fruitiness of dried figs and apricots, a dry blast of chilli, cumin, and fresh coriander; the Mediterranean flavours of olives and lemons - Absolute Bliss!

My preference of meat is either skinned chicken thigh or leg of lamb, diced and marinated with that holy trinity of spice, garlic, ginger, and chilli, with the addition of salt, pepper, and lemon juice. If you can prepare it in advance, just throw all of these things into a large food bag and leave in the fridge for 48 hours (squish around every now and then). If you don't have the fresh garlic, ginger, chilli – on this occasion the dry option will do!

Forget the dried apricots and those overpriced mini salted lemons! Just pre-soak a couple of handfuls of sultanas in a little boiling water until plump. Blitz two large onions in the food processor until fairly liquid, then bring the onion to a low simmer in a saucepan and add fresh garlic, several teaspoons of cumin, a similar volume of dried coriander leaf and, finally, a few tablespoons of tomato purée. Cook out the spice for several minutes, stirring often. Add stock, a tin of tomatoes, a regular lemon chopped into cubes and de-seeded, and those plump sultanas you soaked earlier. That is the perfect stock for your 'Taste of North Africa'. I would fry off my marinated meat at this point and when lightly browned, add to the stock pot with a few handfuls of stoned olives - black or green, you choose. After ten minutes or so on a low simmer, I add a few carrots, peeled and cut lengthwise into quarters. After another ten minutes I add a couple of courgettes, also cut lengthwise and quartered. fifteen more minutes, test your vegetables, you don't want them over cooked now do you? Finally check for seasoning.

Accompany your delicious, aromatic, sumptuous delight with couscous. Just boil the kettle and dissolve two Knorr vegetable or chicken stock cubes in a bowl. Add a handful or two of pre-soaked sultanas and fifty percent dry couscous to the volume of liquid. Leave to stand for five minutes and add roughly chopped coriander leaf before serving. Finally search Spotify for some suitably sounding Moroccan belly dancing music - play very loudly, and enjoy!

Chapter Eleven
August

"Our bodies contain three grams of iron, three grams of bright, silver-white magnesium, and smaller amounts of manganese and copper. Proportionate to size, they are among the weightiest atoms in our bodies, and they come from the same source, a long-ago star. There are pieces of star within us all."
— Vincent Cronin, The View from Planet Earth

The Summer holidays were truly upon us. The days slipped into one another and became a little 'samey' from day to day. Breakfast, lunch and dinner were always at the same time for the children as we have always felt that it's best to have a routine with them. We tried to do arts and crafts in the mornings, something to keep the creative juices flowing and try to hold their interest, maybe baking or painting. There was usually a trip out in the afternoons, weather permitting; maybe a visit to the park to feed the ducks and have an hour in the playground, or a trip to a local farm – one that's open to the public, obviously! If the weather wasn't too good, then maybe some television or an hour or so on their tablets, or reading and writing practice. Weekends were always a little crazier, as you know, what with Daddy at home and Sindy not here.

A couple of weeks before we were due to go on holiday, we got the not so famous five to try on their wetsuits to make sure they hadn't grown out of them, and let them play in the pool to check for leaks; thankfully they all fit well enough, and were still waterproof enough, to do for the holiday. As we got closer to the trip to Cornwall the excitement amongst them was ramping up! Every time Sindy or I went into one of the bedrooms, one or more of the not so famous five had pulled clothes from drawers and wardrobes and dumped them on the floor in order to choose what to pack! I lost count of the number of times we put the dratted clothes away, only to find them out again, and garments thrown into suitcases any which way!

Sadly, the weekend before we were due to leave, John lost his mother after a long battle with cancer. His sisters Sara and Judy were with her throughout her fight, along with her husband, Michael. Although it wasn't unexpected, we were all incredibly sad that she had gone, and my thoughts were with John's family who had selflessly been at vigil those past weeks. Rest in peace Hazel, mother to John and granny to our crew...

The funeral was on the Wednesday; John had already gone over and I flew to Dublin to join him on the Tuesday. We felt it wouldn't be wise to bring our five; they were still a bit too young and chaotic to understand, of course, so Sindy would be staying with them in our absence.

Before I left, I explained to all of them that Daddy and Dadda were going to Ireland to say our goodbyes to Granny Hazel, and I think they realise that a funeral is the place for people to do that.

The little ones don't really comprehend her passing, but Tara and Amritsar knew that Granny Hazel had been gravely ill and deserved an explanation of why we needed to say goodbye to her. I started with a chat with Amritsar on the terrace the day after Hazel died. I opened the conversation with 'We are all made of stars.'

Now, I am not that religious and honesty, I find, works best! I spoke about the cosmos and the way that 'matter' will always remain within it, that we are all made of stars and that some people believe that nature, like the cosmos, will always reclaim us! I also explained that some people believe in heaven... It probably sounded a bit pitiful, but I think they realise we are never fully gone!

We went in and talked with Tara and I said that granny had died. Tara, the more empathetic of them, cried. We hugged a lot, there were more tears and more hugs, followed by my suggestion that it might be appropriate to eat ice cream. The girls agreed and that was that. We also bought a book written to help younger children to understand and deal with the death of a loved one, so hopefully that will explain it all a bit better than I could.

My mum, Grandma Jean, passed away almost four years ago, and I think we dealt with remembering her very well. Although they were babies when she died, her memory and spirit are always with us. When the girls were two years old, she visited us from Australia where she lived. A few photos of the girls with her helped tremendously; there is one of them in pink dresses with my mother, who was wearing multi coloured earrings. The girls were playing with those earrings in the pictures, and it's a treasured memory. We now have those earrings in the drawer of the game's cupboard, and every so often we play with them and the girls wear them and look at the photos of her on my phone. I might just get them printed out.

We really must do the same with the memory of Granny Hazel. Forever in our thoughts.

Six days into our summer holiday and the weather had been foul; the dratted rain had not stopped! I believe it was the greyest week on record! Our holiday home was nestled in the dunes, so our visits to the beach had been daily, whatever the weather; we'd seen our fair share of sand and had pretty much moved into the shower.

The little ones were a bit stir crazy because of the weather and had been a wee bit destructive; a chair and the dining table were badly scraped, plus the living room wall had been deeply scratched by Caleb. We ventured out to Barnstable one day, to Homebase, to buy Polyfilla and a spatula, plus a sample pot of a light sage green paint, almost indistinguishable from the original. Fingers were crossed on that score otherwise our substantial deposit would not have been refunded!

The children had been a little chaotic from time to time and decided that 9 p.m. was their new bedtime, which meant that for about an hour before they actually ventured into the bedrooms, they were running rings around the living room, pulling cushions off the sofa and throwing them around, and, for instance, pulling each other's pyjama bottoms down and giggling. That poor sofa was used as a trampoline, the back of it was ridden like a horse, it was covered in soft toys and continually climbed over. All to music! Once they were actually in bed and settled John and I spent twenty minutes tidying up and putting the house to rights. Of course, not being a 'school night' and being on holiday, we allowed them a few extra freedoms, and ice cream had been consumed by all on a daily basis. I remember looking in the mirror and seeing the bulge! I will need to re-engage with the weekly fitness regime on my return to The Shires! John, like the children, seems to have a very high metabolism, so he doesn't need to worry on that score.

The sun eventually started to shine, those dratted grey clouds dissipated and the wind had finally been quelled. At last we enjoyed some pleasant summer days at the seaside! The sandy beach was wide and flat, and the minute the sun came out it was crowded with holiday-makers. We had got the not so famous five some bodyboards and John spent hours with each of them, trying to teach them how to do it; he has the patience of a saint! It was fun, and they loved it; Tara and Amritsar were getting the hang of it but, to be honest, the little ones weren't really! Maybe next year. I was happy that they were all very confident in the water, and there were no tears or tantrums when they were splashed or fell over. Our fun days were all finished off with various flavoured ice cream cones, sitting at the tables outside the beach café.

Taking them out to eat wasn't so successful though, and I think that we will limit restaurant visits for the little ones, at least until they start to understand that screaming in shops and restaurants is really quite unacceptable! I am really hoping that 'Big School' turns around their tantrums, at least in public places where people deserve a pleasant time on the likes of their holidays. We all work throughout the year to deserve ourselves a good time when we set off on our hols to relax, don't we? Anyhow, we went to the local supermarket and stocked up; the kitchen was adequate enough to make simple meals, and we picnicked at the garden table for the rest of the holiday.

Once the weather improved, the second week was great fun. We met up with some friends, Kayla and Jamie, who also have twins, and we had a hectic but enjoyable time of it with three sets of twins and Thor, playing games on the beach, building sandcastles, and running in and out of the sea. Sindy came for a few days and John and I grabbed a little time out.

The couple of nights we had alone, thanks to Sindy, were spent eating out, chatting, and generally unwinding with delicious food and wine – and fascinating conversation, obviously!

On the Thursday we feasted at 'Steins' in Padstow; the restaurant is famous for having the freshest fish and shellfish, landed almost on their doorstep! There's a seafood bar right in the middle of the restaurant, and we watched the chefs artistically assembling platters of oysters, langoustines and sashimi. The food was simple, but with classic flavours – absolutely delicious, and what a treat!

On Saturday we ate at 'The Pig' at Combe, a charming honey-coloured Elizabethan country house; the menu changes regularly but there is always locally-reared meat accompanied by fresh vegetables from their famous kitchen garden, the very best Devonshire cheeses, and superb desserts served with luxurious Devon cream. I could feel that the pounds were piling on, and vowed again to get back to my exercising as soon as we were home.

We rounded off our holiday with two nights in East Devon with our friends Alistair and Lorna, who we'd last met up with in October when we had spent a weekend with them.

Fortunately for us they have a swimming pool with a slide, and the not so famous five had a brilliant time sliding down the chute into the clear blue water, over and over, and gaining in confidence with every go. John stayed in the pool with them for the whole time, catching them at the end of the slide to start with, and then standing back and letting them slide under the water, and each time one of them launched off the end and splashed into the pool, we all let out a huge cheer. Mind you, Thor was more intent on learning to swim properly, he happily doggy paddled backwards and forwards for ages. All of the children were, of course, still wearing life vests, but I think that this time next year they will be competent enough to do away with them.

Back at The Shires, the children were still enjoying their summer holidays after our fun, yet exhausting time in Cornwall.

I was away from home on the Friday night, and I returned on Saturday to stories of theft! It seems that after the children had gone to bed, an exhausted Daddy fell asleep on the sofa in front of the television. Two opportunistic thieves, namely Tara and Thor, descended the stairs and sneaked past the open living room door, where they stopped momentarily and observed daddy snoozing; they continued on their stealthy journey to the kitchen, and surveyed the area for booty.

Everyone else in the house was sound asleep and all was quiet; when they awoke the following morning, Aaliyah found a squashed flat peach stuck to her bum (not pleasant!) and when Caleb discovered the same, he devoured the surprise manna with gusto. Amritsar did the right thing and gave hers to our daddy to return it to the fruit bowl. Tara and Thor said that they were sorry for their actions...

The story continued; later, whilst cooking their dinner, I looked for dessert options. The cupboard was bare on that front so I ventured into the housekeeper's cupboard where lies (in a bag) several chocolate bars and a dozen mini packs of Haribo fruit gums. One of the 200g chocolate bars was open and half nibbled and four of the Haribo packets were emptied of their contents! It also seemed that the peach that Amritsar had replaced in the bowl had also, once again, been stolen. Nobody came forward to confess to these crimes, so at dinner, when it came to dessert, I placed the half-eaten chocolate bar and empty sweet packets on the table. Tara and Thor were quite bold as both declined to comment on the matter. When I said that there would be no dessert due to the situation, Caleb decided to hurl his drinking cup towards me. Thankfully the cup was empty, and his aim is not that great anyway, so he missed!

'Okay, that's it!' I exclaimed. 'Off to bed, everyone.'

Lots of screaming and a few 'Sorry Dadda's' later, they all marched up to bed. I don't really have a 'summing up' of the situation. But I hope that my decision to send them up to bed resonates in the form of the guilty parties not doing it again as it does affect everybody – doesn't it?

In the vegetable garden, this year's crop of tomatoes, courgettes and peppers were looking good, very colourful and healthy, and almost ready to pick. It involves an awful lot of watering and attention for a single meal of ratatouille though! I'm not sure that I will bother next year. Mind you I say this every year, but then give in and plant them again! And I have to admit, they do taste amazing, much more bursting with flavour – little explosions on the tongue - than the blander shop-bought offerings.

The terrace continued to be rather active on the bird nest front, with plenty of comings and goings and chirping! I imagine the chicks will be fully-fledged and ready to leave the nest soon enough, probably about the same time that our little ones will be ready to leave our own 'nest' and start at 'Big School'.

The Perfect Ratatouille

For something so simple, I cannot believe that so few of us make this a weekly treat! Today's recipe is 'Ratatouille'. A taste of Provence that will get your taste buds tingling and fill you to the brim with great nutrition. As a vegetarian meal option, this has to be up there with another of our family favourites, puttanesca! Ratatouille can be served with pasta, but also goes great with Dadda's torn potatoes or just a simple green salad. If serving with pasta, warm slightly, but mark my words - serve at room temperature on all other occasions. I think that the flavours permeate the palate so much better when heat is omitted.

Okay, today's rendition is intensified with our August crop of courgettes, tomatoes, sweet capsicum and silver skin onions. Did I forget the aubergine? Firstly, we did not grow any, and secondly, I never use them in this dish! I think a few of you will agree - they are not essential. The shop-purchased items are half a tube of tomato purée, some crushed garlic and salt and pepper to taste!

The method is too simple to even mention, but I would state that personally I would cut my onion and capsicum in medium to large chunks and sauté them in a little oil first; when softened, add the sliced courgettes. Stir from time to time, then turn the heat down to the lowest setting and place a lid on the pan. Check again in ten minutes or so, and add plenty of garlic and seasoning. Give it a stir and turn up the heat slightly. When the pan starts to sizzle, add your skinned tomatoes, break them down a bit with the wooden spoon you are using, then add the purée. Cook for a further ten minutes, stirring from time to time. Check for seasoning and – voila! Cool in the pan, then store in the fridge for up to five days.

If you are skinning your own tomatoes, I have one small tip for you, and that is - forget the 'cheffy' way with a cross cut into the bottom of the tomato and pop into boiling water. It's so much simpler to just quarter them, place on a microwaveable plate or dish, and blitz them for a few minutes. Cool a little and you can then peel the skin away with ease.

Chapter Twelve
September

"Stay Happy. And the Moon and the stars will shine forever."
— Anthony T. Hincks

The first week of September and the terrace had finally fallen silent with not a single flapping wing or chirp to be heard. The song thrushes have finally flown from their nest. They were a committed duo doing their best to protect and nourish their little family until they were fully fledged and ready to fly away and make their own way in the world. Fitting I thought, what with our little ones about to do just that! The terrace didn't seem the same. But the lesson I learnt from this loving, mated pair, is that perseverance pays dividends.

The Sunday before the little ones started Big School for the first time, we had a chaotic time making Baby Boxes. John and I had bought five large cardboard boxes, flat-packed, so we constructed them and gave one to each child, complete with their name written on the side. And then the fun began!

The walk-in wardrobe in our bedroom was stacked with dozens of bags and boxes that contained hundreds of baby and toddler items, Babygro's, rattles, teething rings, toys, books – you name it, it was there! One by one the boxes and bags were emptied onto the carpet in the middle of the room and it was reminiscent of a jumble sale as little hands rummaged and grabbed familiar items. They played with the toys, tried on the clothes – much too small now, of course – and argued about which belonged to who! Caleb had a little wobble when he found a small yellow and white dress that had belonged to Aaliyah and wanted to keep it for himself. I let him keep the matching mop cap, but next time I turned around he was wearing the dress, which looked more like a t-shirt! Thor was parading around in an old pair of pyjamas, crying because his wind-up baby mobile wouldn't work, Aaliyah ran in circles with a musical book and a plastic drinking cup, and Tara and Amritsar divided up some of their old toys in quite a mature fashion. There were piles of folders, from pre-school, containing reports and early drawings. Stainless steel tiffin boxes (curry tins) that I'd brought from Goa went into Amritsar and Tara's boxes, baby blankets were discovered with delight, and all of them had a copy of my book, Eighteen Moons (which, in case you are wondering, is available on Amazon!). There were mugs that each of them had decorated, tea towels with their handprints on – so many memories went into those baby boxes, and they were to be kept closed for at least fifteen years!

Amritsar and Tara returned to 'Big School' a few days before the three little ones, and Sindy left for her annual holiday at the weekend. On the Monday morning, getting five of them washed and breakfasted, and into their school uniforms, was confusing as five sets of shirts, shoes, jumpers, and ties, all became somewhat muddled. We managed to sort out the correct uniform for each child, and they each managed to do their own buttons and ties, although Thor's was askew and showing the dratted label on the outside! John brushed the girls' hair and tied them up with ribbons, and they were all ready at last! The obligatory first-day photographs were taken, one with them seated on the sofa, and one of them lined up outside the front door shouting 'Chocolate Cheesecake,' which always produces a smile! We had been counting down the days, and on that momentous occasion both John and I did the school run. John was working from home for two weeks in

Sindy's absence. We found the whole morning emotional, and it was very strange to leave them all at school and go back to an empty house.

The children had flown the nest!

Where did the time go? It seems to have been non-stop for the last six years and on that first day of school for all of them together, I found myself at odds with what to do with my new-found freedom! Okay, things were busy first thing, but as soon as John and I returned home, the house seemed unusually quiet. John was working from home so he was busy in the office.

I headed down the driveway and gathered blackberries, then I went up to the orchard to pick apples for making pectin. You got it; Dadda's Jam was going to play a part in my new-found free time. I didn't know if it was something I might start to focus on again; it has been a constant these last few years, since the little ones started preschool, but six hours every day need to be filled somehow! How does 'Blackberry Cider' Jam grab you? Alongside the already infamous 'Blue Cherry Berry' Jam! Woohoo, I think we have a winner!

I kept myself busy Jammin' and the time really flew; suddenly it was home time! We collected the not so famous five from school, and from the minute we met them we were flooded with stories of their first day, excitedly talking over one another, none of them making much sense until we questioned what they meant. I was intrigued! They have a whole new life outside of the home that doesn't include John or myself, and they are meeting new people, teachers, peers, that we don't really know. It was a strange feeling, one that, I'm sure, every parent of a school-aged child has experienced, and I will be studying any changes in the little ones' behaviour!

On their second morning Caleb was rather shy at the school doorway. A little girl from one of the older years made it her place to talk to him and reassure him that school was a good thing! Praise to her! Aaliyah, on the other hand, went straight in the doors and hung up her coat and P.E. Kit. Thor, like Caleb was cautious, but found his confidence quick enough.

Back at home I sat on the terrace with a coffee. All was quiet, except for the tap, tap, tapping of the red-headed woodpecker from somewhere within the foliage of the red-leafed plum tree. It reminded me that Caleb was in the school house/team called Woodpeckers. John had gone off to get a pane of glass cut to replace the broken window of the shed at the bottom of the garden, hidden behind the mass of overgrown rhododendrons.

I decided, on my second day of 'freedom', that I would be productive. I took the Aga apart and gave it a good clean, leaving the bits to dry by the sink while I sorted out two bags of a random collection of broken plastic toys that were destined for the rubbish bin. Remus and Gracie were chilled on the sofa, with daytime television doing its thing in the background. I usually leave it on to settle the dogs, even when I'm not in the room. I think that I have mentioned the way in which Remus strains to hear sounds that he can have a good bark at. I had a general tidy up around the house, put the Aga back together, and made yet another new combo for 'Dadda's Jam'. How does Plum and Calvados sound? Drizzled over Haagen Das vanilla ice cream with dark chocolate shavings maybe? Not for the children, of course, but rather Daddy and Dadda's dessert that night!

This new chapter in my life might need some fine-tuning. It's very quiet on weekdays for me, what with all of the children at school. It might take a few weeks to find my new direction. Though with me not driving, I still feel a little housebound. I think they say 'do what you know' but I'm not sure what I do know anymore! The family has been everything to me these last six years.

I should have known it was too good to last! On the third morning at school drop-off, Amritsar and Tara had very lovingly given us both massive hugs and kissed us goodbye, then marched through the door to their welcoming teachers on the opposite side of the yard. Aaliyah very excitedly skipped into the cloakroom area, full of smiles, and I could see her happily locating her own hook and hanging up her coat and bag. But Thor clung to my leg, sobbing, then Caleb joined in, neither of them wanted to enter the cloakroom area where Aaliyah had disappeared just moments before. Shortly after, it was Daddy's leg, then mine again, then the breakdown happened. Both Thor and Caleb screamed; they sobbed like it was the end of the world, with gulping and runny noses! The other parents looked on, a few with looks of disbelief at the shenanigans that were in action. The reception year teacher and the TA did what they could to calm the situation and distract the boys, and I indicated to John that we should make a speedy getaway! Ellie, one of the friendly mums at the gate gave us a few words of support.

I guess we were lucky that the separation issues waited until day three of Big School. The boys generally settle after ten minutes or so, and I knew they are in very safe hands. John was going to have to do the drop off on his own on day four, so I hoped all would go well. The children play up for daddy that bit more than with me as they don't see him as often and they compete for his attentions! That coupled with Thor loving an audience. Humph...

With time on my hands, and what with me scuttling around trying to complete the contents of our not so famous five's 'Baby Boxes', I decided to clear out the shelf of one of our wardrobes. My mission was to thin out all of the physical items that were part of our family's early experiences. It seems that from both India and Thailand, I kept every single receipt, invoice, airline boarding pass and document that ever passed through my hands. The important documents that we needed in order to gain British passports and Exit Visas were already filed away for all of our children, but all of those little incidentals, passport photos, bits of stationery, you name it, were surveyed and sorted.

All of those monthly accommodation invoices – bin. All of those small trinkets – priceless. I had hotel key cards for the Novotel in Juhu Beach, where I started this journey. Then on to the Marriott Executive Apartments in Powai, Bombay (there were other unmentionable accommodations) and then onto the Marriott apartments in Bangkok, Thailand. Nothing on that score from Nepal however as we stayed in regular apartments at - dare I say - relatively overinflated prices! Indian, Thai and Nepalese mobile Sim Cards were all there, Bangkok sky train tickets. In fact, so many small reminders and memories of those 'Eighteen Moons' spent far away from home had certainly mounted up over that time.

There were also documents reminding me of some bizarre and some not so happy moments. There was the invoice and covering letter from the 'Hiranandani Hospital' (where the girls were born) at around seven months into our prolonged stay in Mumbai. I had a breakdown due to the extreme circumstances that were holding us in stasis. Nothing to worry about I was told, just anxiety – a form of panic attack. It was a completely distressing and upsetting time. I felt really emotional when I uncovered an independent doctor's prescription and the diagnosis letter that he wrote - it stated that I was suffering from a deep depression; I needed that letter to show to the Indian authorities, to enable me to return home with Tara and Amritsar. I was so grateful for their diagnosis as I could not have imagined being side-lined from the girls for a single moment in those, our darkest hours!

I was particularly looking for two pieces of material swatches that were our nanny Bharti's old torn saris that she used to swaddle our little babes as they slept in their early months of life. We have seen the girls in swaddling in various photographs and now these relative rags are destined to be a lifetime memory, but just for now, to be hidden away in the children's 'Baby Boxes!'

Certainly, a day of mixed emotions and memories for me. Even a tear or two was shed!

Thank you to our friends Victoria and Glen, and their daughter Fi, for making the weekend such a great one. This Brighton duo are an absolute pleasure to see. Just their daughter Fi was in tow as their other two older children, Lucy and Aiden had their own stuff going on, but I think she got on with our girls fairly well – you know, they all rubbed along very well and didn't scream too loudly whilst running around like crazies! It was to Brighton that John and I ventured earlier in the year for the wedding of Glen and Victoria.

Saturday night was another excuse for Dadda to cook curry (five different kinds!) and on Sunday Daddy insisted on cooking the leg of lamb dinner (I can't remember the last time John cooked!). It was well executed, thank you John, though I had to lend a hand to magic-up a nut-roast as both Victoria and Fi are Vegetarians.

Okay, we drank way too much on the Saturday night, but you have to do that when you see old friends and the children are snuggled up in bed don't you?

Sunday saw us all invade the woodlands nearby. The weather was great and the dogs all began to get on well. Did I mention that Remus's son Fenton is part of Victoria and Glens family? Gracie being a bit of a bully at times wasn't the nicest of sisters to poor old Fenton, but I think they ended the weekend on good terms!

Before we knew it, it was time for them to go home! Thank you so much guys. Let's not leave it too long before another catch-up.

On Sunday night, when John and I thought the not so famous five were all tucked up in bed, Tara took it upon herself to give her brothers and sisters 'a quick trim!' I wouldn't have minded so much, but they had been to the hairdresser in the last few weeks, giving them all the perfect haircut. I knew nothing of her antics, obviously, until the next day.

So, on Monday morning, when hurriedly putting the girls' hair up into ponytails for school, something seemed odd! I couldn't quite put my finger on it – did all five children have more of a fringe than I remembered? Surely not! In the chaos of getting them all ready for school, I put the idea out of my mind.

However, that evening, the penny dropped, and I realised something was indeed, very out of kilter. Now, a parent's power of deduction, coupled with question time for them all, soon led to finding out exactly what had happened and who the culprit was.

Somehow, Tara had smuggled up to their bedrooms a pair of child-safe scissors. She cut a part of her own fringe down to one centimetre, and it will take maybe two years to regrow her beautiful black locks. Amritsar said that Tara sneaked up on her whilst she was reading a book in bed; she cut her fringe by several inches so it might take a year or so to grow back. Caleb, Aaliyah and Thor were happy participants though! Thor would benefit from a number-two crew cut to even up the length. Caleb had the least damage inflicted, but poor Aaliyah! Her hair has been the slowest to grow of all of our children, yet she is now going to have to wait at least another year for her fine blonde ringlets to grow back to the length they were; her splendid hair had certainly added to her outward beauty.

I am just so unhappy that all of our children's fringes will all take such a long time to grow out, absolutely devastated with what Tara has created. I really do hate telling her off as she is usually the most perfect angel, but just how do you teach an angel to be good, and to scrutinise when they have done something wrong? She is certainly no fallen angel, she accepts when she has done wrong, and will certainly never reoffend after her lessons have been learnt. I do so hate being upset with Tara. She is a 'Big Sister' and should know better, but I really was very upset with the situation...

There was a mega breakdown at the school gate the next afternoon! And just who would you imagine had the breakdown? To be honest, there were a number of mini meltdowns by both Thor and Caleb after they had exited from their classroom. The emotional traumas were mostly associated with the PTFA selling ice-cream and lollies in the school yard. I knew it would lead to trouble. I said to John 'This will lead to trouble,' and guess what? It led to trouble!

There were complete screamy tantrums from both Caleb (having dropped his ice cream within minutes), then

Thor, mostly venting his unjustified anger, running around like a thunderstorm, preparing his little bolts of lightning and energised screams of thunder for all the waiting mums and dads to endure.

In the end Daddy had to pick him up and put him under his arm in order to get him to the car, but his tantrum continued; if anything, he got louder and louder and so very angry. Legs were kicking and his high-pitched screaming was his very vocal contribution to this afternoon's drama in the school yard. Caleb had settled once his ice cream had been replaced; I couldn't believe that Caleb might have been considered possible competition to Thor's starring role in what can only be explained as hellish! A moment that was extremely upsetting for both Daddy and Dadda.

It wasn't a good end to Thor's second week at 'Big School.' I only hope that with our nanny Sindy's return on Monday, his behaviour settles. There's no going back. But I have to hope that Thor will adapt, in time...

I'm sure that all parents will agree that you don't like your child to be unhappy, but you also have to note when a child decides to bring you down a peg or two (usually with an audience!). It is very upsetting.

Well, thanks to the 'scream time' there's to be no 'screen time' for the foreseeable – I'm looking for a little more 'Harmony in the Home' before Thor enjoys his 'Crossy Road' again!

Not only was Saturday the Autumn Equinox, it was also forecast to be the last day of summery weather for this year, so we bundled the not so famous five into the car and headed for the Berkshire County Show. It really was shorts and t-shirt weather. We took a picnic along to enjoy before we took advantage of the funfair. All of them were excited and couldn't wait to get onto the rides. But which one to go on first?

The Carousel beckoned, its colourful horses elegantly soaring upwards, and gently down again, in a graceful arc; the three girls clambered onto the horses' backs, with a little help from Daddy, and Tara and Aaliyah were strapped on securely; Amritsar was the only one who did not use a strap on the Carousel - how very grown up of her! Caleb and Thor chose to go into the little carriage; Daddy helped them do up their seat belts, and they were away! Fairground organ music played loudly, lights twinkled, and the children laughed with excitement, waving to us each time they whooshed past.

The Helter-Skelter came next, that tall twisty slide so beloved of children. Coir mats in hand, Tara and Amritsar went first, followed by Thor, then Aaliyah and finally Daddy with Caleb on his knees. The slide down on the mat was quite fast, they all squealed with delight. Daddy also loved it!

The baby-big-wheel was a success too, and as each of them swooped down and past us they waved and shouted, laughing and kicking their legs – they really liked it, although Aaliyah had a momentary wobble, but was fine again immediately. I had to laugh at Thor though; there was a look of pure joy on his face as he swept past and screamed at us 'I love it!'

Amritsar and Tara were then harnessed onto large bungee ropes which helped them jump ever higher on a huge trampoline, while the rest of us watched in awe, shouting encouragement. I think, though, that the highlight of the day was for them to get to sit in a real police car. All five of them climbed in and strapped up, with Tara in the driving seat; I just prayed they wouldn't get too carried away and break something, because then I would probably get carried away - by the policemen that stood by, watching very closely!

On Monday, Sindy was back from her travels and resumed the school run. This allowed Daddy to return to work, and for me to once again get Jammin' – and by home-time several jars of Dadda's Damson Jam, Mint Jelly, and Crab-apple Jelly, were lined up in the cupboard. When Sindy said goodnight to the children she said just how much they were missed, and they settled happily. Normal service had been resumed!

It was late summer when we met up with some of the teaching staff, and they gave us three sparkly, reflective cut-outs of hot-air balloons with which to make collages for each of the little ones, showing what they had got up to during the summer. The collages were to be handed in at school, duly finished, so, of course, it was me that ended up chopping up photographs (the printer was still not working!) and frantically sticking a few – a lot when you have to do it three times! - of our summertime memories onto the balloons.

I believe that when all thirteen children in the class have finished their project (or rather, when their parents have found the time!), they will be talking about their summer holidays to the rest of their class. These memory balloons will be stuck to the wall at school for the next few months, but when they return home, we will have a small piece of time standing still to include in their future reminders of childhood. Definitely something for the Baby Box's 'additional items' box. Tara and Amritsar's balloons are somewhere in the wardrobe!

I was just thinking how big the 'additions' box might end up being! Maybe we should attach the balloons to the tops of the actual baby boxes since they are sealed for the next fifteen years? Now there's an idea! I smiled at my brilliance!

It seems that every household has a routine, and with Sindy back from her holidays, and the not so famous five at school, things were beginning to settle into a 'new' normal. I had been busy making dozens of jars of various chutneys and jams, and the provisions cupboard was practically bursting at the seams, but I was still on the lookout for a new 'project.' I considered learning to drive and, alongside John, lots of my friends thought I should do just that. I was also thinking about a business manoeuvre regarding 'Dadda's Jam' and seeing if a third party (a large long-established company) might be interested in licensing 'Dadda's Jam' as a brand, and sexing-up the Jam industry a little. You know, get away from the frumpy, old lady image of it! But sadly, the concept fell on deaf ears.

So, with so many funky combos, I've decided that my next project may have to be another book. Not just any book, but a recipe book containing all of Dadda's 'Jammy Combos'. Mind you, I know nothing of compiling a glossy, commercial recipe book for Jams and Chutneys, but I am going to get working on *Dadda Gets Jammin'* very soon – I can't wait!

The last few days of September, and Autumn had surely arrived; the temperature dropped several degrees, and the wind had the first fall of orange and brown leaves swirling and dancing on the lawn. On Sunday evening television, Countryfile was competing with Strictly come Dancing – the only show that's camper than Christmas! This week saw the children find a frog stuck in the neck of the watering can, then today two newts were discovered in the brown grass/moss beneath the now emptied swimming pool. Lots of eggs were also there. A neighbour helped carefully move them to their pond, where I believe there is a small population already surviving the rigours of the British elements.

There were many crazy runs around the living room and kitchen over the weekend, as the not so famous five burned off excess energy. The games cupboard was completely emptied at one point, and hopefully some of the multiple pieces from those various games and puzzles are back in their correct boxes. My rule – one game at a time – was totally ignored by John!

I spent some time Jammin' in the kitchen, making this year's 'Xmas X-rated' Jam. A delicious combination of rum-soaked raisins, pears, sugar, an extra slug of rum, apple pulp and lemon juice, all this complemented with a combination of fragrant, festive spices. A real indulgence and the aromatics should be well infused in their sterilised jars by the time Xmas arrives. Regular strawberry jam was also made this week plus a well-set raspberry jelly, sieved to exclude the pips, and the perfect marriage to thickly buttered sour dough toast.

For Gracie, a run in the morning dew led to a slow limp back to me on the terrace, her eyes saddened. On looking down I noticed a little blood and her 'dew claw' bent at a 90-degree angle. Poor Gracie, she yelped when I touched it. We had the inevitable trip to the vet who, essentially, just snapped the dew claw off, no local anaesthetic at all and charged us £50 for the privilege! Gracie was not happy but seems to have cheered up now, a couple of treats and hugs later! Though having said that, the vet suggested Gracie should go on a diet as she is five kilos overweight. Better cut down on the treats I guess, but it seems unfair to give one to Remus (who burns off the calories) and not one to Gracie. Other than that, all is well.

An easy nut-roast recipe for you now, and one that I hope Victoria (Jeary) will have a go at as she seemed to enjoy it!

I used cashew nuts, but peanuts are fine. Also, I chose dried mushrooms from my provision's cupboard; they absorb liquid well when it comes to cooking in combination with ingredients that are better with a dry consistency, such as nut-loaf or rissoles (nut balls).

Just mince two or three onions in the food processor, leave aside. Do the same with the cashew nuts, then the mushrooms (fresh are fine). You don't need measurements, just play it by ear. A little more or less of this or that is fine! I would only add that you shouldn't overdo the breadcrumbs. I toasted two pieces of sliced bread and left them to cool, then blitzed the two slices into oblivion, that was ample for a medium sized loaf for four. Mix all of the dry ingredients together with a little salt and pepper, a little water or stock and pack into an oiled loaf tin and cook at about 160 degrees for 35 minutes. Come to think of it – walnuts really rock in this recipe too.

Okay, a reflection on this month! This will conclude my edit from my Diary of a Gay Dad, just shy of one year old. This year was a fitting one to note as it was the year leading up to the younger children fledging the nest. There were quite a few ups and quite a few downs as well throughout the year. But it is important to add that we are just a regular family, nothing more, nothing less to what any of you guys out there experience. Some of my memories you will probably recognise from your own family experiences and others, maybe you will just smile or possibly sympathise with.

As a committed couple both John and I love all of our children deeply. I was initially unsure on whether to adapt my online diary blog into a paperback book. Unlike Eighteen Moons, a fascinating, unusual story of how we became a family, there is nothing however unusual about living life here in The Shires of England. But then I thought it would be fitting to show you a slice of who we are today, what became of us and where we are going. My 2-year, online diary archive is still live at andiwebb.net or diaryofagaydad.net so maybe look in there from time to time. There are occasional updates and you can see how we are all doing. That's it for now from me, John and our not so famous five.

This is Andi Webb, signing off...

Printed in Great Britain
by Amazon